THREE GENERATIONS IN TOBACCO

THREE GENERATIONS IN TOBACCO

Shehui Guhua and Populist Autocracy in Communist China

Dongmei Jing Tang

This Book is dedicated to

The 2600 protestors who died and all who were wounded at Tiananmen.

To the Hong Kong 47, including Benny Tai and Jimmy Lai, whose only crime was that they supported the principles of Democracy by legally submitting an alternate slate of election candidates.

And finally, to 'Tank Man', who confirmed the humanity, courage and innate commitment to freedom possessed by the average Chinese citizen. Hopefully one day soon the world will know your name.

And to:

Eric Hoffer, the most consequential Political Philosopher of the 20th Century, whose seminal work 'The True Believer' was used as a foundation for this book.

ISBN: 9798303840454
Imprint: D3 Publishing and Media Corporation
~2_6~

About the Author

Ms. Tang has a degree in Political Science and an MBA from two large American Universities.

She can be reached at DongmeiJingTang@gmail.com

Or visit DTSTB.com

"The dragon gives birth to a Dragon, the Phoenix gives birth to a Phoenix, and the rat's son knows how to dig"

Chinese Proverb

Contents

PREFACE

Conspiracies are the Black Holes of Truth. They are much studied but never understood. This book will attempt to lend clarity to the irrational, a hall mark of all political systems, but one that claims a peculiar place of prominence in Communist propagandistic theory, and which is now used in China to rationalize a return to isolation and social control. The most powerful weapon known to Man is the lie. After all the human capacity to rationalize knows no bounds, and when unleashed by Pride and Power can be used to legitimize unspeakable acts in the name of redeeming past grievances and restoring manifest destiny to Nations as ordained by racial and cultural imperatives.

We see this in America and Europe, and now in the gradual retrenchment that China has experienced in the three generations of Paramount Leaders since Deng Xiaoping. The third is no longer Communist. He has morphed into an Absolutist, an Authoritarian and Autocrat, who uses the lexicon of Nationalist Populism to tighten his grip on Party and Populous. He has taken the endemic historical pride of China, and of the Chinese

People in the Open Door Policy initiated by Deng Xiaoping, and turned it inward using a hubristic program that has the potential to resurrect the caricature of progress that was Mao's Great Leap Forward.

An inclination to look inward in order to aggrandize political legitimacy is not an historical Chinese cultural motivation, but rather springs from all political movements led by Populists. It is an affect that is growing in Europe, and which has now metastasized in America in the sewer that is American multi-media and the political tumor that is Donald Trump. It is a lazy attempt to manipulate the populous by using a perverted appeal to Nationalism.

In China this new inclination to take 2 steps back in order to move 1 step forward harkens back to the "Edict of Haijin" issued by Emperor Xuande in 1434, which banned most overseas trade and interactions, essentially isolating China from international commerce and exploration: a policy motivated by concerns about piracy and managing economic pressures with neighboring countries like Japan. It of course was also the inflection point that led to the waning of China's impact on history that would come to a final eruption in the genocide and tragedy of Mao's Great Leap Forward. It was a multi-generational wasting of the intellectual energy and capacity for innovation that left China vulnerable to the crime of imperialism and bereft of a capacity to resist Japanese fascist aggression. Pride and vengeance now threaten China's willingness to engage the World productively as an independent but complementary member of the global community.

The challenge for World Governments will be to understand that China needs to be understood in terms of the bifurcating pull of extra-national cultural diversity and prosperity, and the constricting call for sacrifice and compliance as dictated by an appeal to abrogate self-determination in the name of a single people dedicated to a communal Republic.

When this sacrifice is looked at using the descriptions of fanaticism provided by Eric Hoffer in 'The True Believer', I believe a framework can be created that not only explains their incurious support of President Jinping, but that can also be used as a basis for how to effectively counter and prevent the gestation of Autocratic Populism and Fascism in Communist China.

The People's Republic is no longer a global pariah. Chinese economic imperialism can be thwarted, but not by isolating the country culturally. Unlike Russia which will continue to be weakened as it continues to engage militarily with Ukraine, President Jinping can only be frustrated by re-engaging the Chinese populous with the rest of the world. Putin's grip will be broken by his waste of Russian treasure in foreign wars. President Jinping's grip can be broken by the allure of an irresistible Chinese yearning to participate in the global cultural experience. Communism cannot survive the bright light of a world dedicated to openness and transparency.

China needs to be induced to continue to open itself to the world so that it and indeed the entire world might benefit and prosper from the innate and mighty power it possesses to innovate and reinvent itself.

That President Jinping is reorienting the country to regain the pride of place he feels it deserves as this planet's pre-eminent nation, which lead China down the path to isolation. That Trump is doing the same in the US implies that the two countries are on an inevitable collision course as they attempt to assert dominance.

What needs to be done is to understand the character of the Chinese Polity, and work to constructively engage the Nation's creative capacity for industry and profit. With it the People will change the Party, and the Party will reorganize in favor of a more inclusive, open, and complementary relationship with the World. The other option is a return to ignorance and isolation, and with it a concomitant propensity for violence of action. The way we engage with China will determine the fate of the Planet. For the World's Democracies, the choice and outcome is ours to make.

PRELUDE 序幕

After a sycophantic reproachment with Trump, followed by Chinese government sponsored 3rd party investments in Trump family-owned cryptocurrencies and real estate projects, Xi decides to make his move. Offshore near Toucheng in Taiwan, a remotely operated submersible drone is launched from China's newest Type 09IIIB nuclear-powered attack submarine. Fiber optic cables are cut. The mission is replicated near Tanshui, Pali, and Fangsha. Satellites are destroyed using multiple ASAT kinetic kill vehicles launched from the Jiuquan Satellite Launch Center (JSLC) located in Gansu Province, some of which had been in orbit since 2023. The American Nusajaya data center in Jahor, Malaysia suffers a mysterious terrorist attack that takes the entire facility offline. Starlink access in Taiwan is denied. Chinese force projection is arrayed around the island, daring US naval forces to respond. Trump will hesitate. China will use his inaction to initiate a blockade of military aid.

Taiwan will challenge the blockade by assigning a Kee Lung (Kidd) class Destroyer supported by two over the horizon capable Kuang Hua VI (Kwang-Hwa)-class missile ships to escort the USN Arctic, 1 of 2 active 49,000-ton supply-class fast combat support ships to port. China's newest Type 055 Stealth Destroyer will radio a warning to desist and then fire a salvo from its single barrel H/PJ-38 130 mm naval gun, damaging but not disabling the Kee Lung Destroyer. As the confrontation escalates a Chinese Xi'an H-6 long range Bomber will fire 4 YJ-83 anti-ship missiles at both the Destroyer and the Merchant Ship. Both will be sunk. The Kwang-Hwa-class missile ships will fire multiple Harpoons at the Chinese Destroyer. It will split in half and sink in minutes. A Taiwanese F-15EX Eagle II will simultaneously fire 2 AIM-174B long range air to air missiles which will destroy the Chinese Badger. At that point the war for the Republic of China will have begun.

Penghu County Island, just 45 kilometers (28 miles) off the coast of Taiwan, is swarmed by 2 newly commissioned type 076 Chinese Amphibious Assault ships. YJ-63 air launched and DH-10 ground launched subsonic cruise missiles will blanket the island and destroy ROC anti-aircraft missile systems. Accompanied by heavy bombing of Taiwanese defensive positions and supported by 2 paratroop brigades, the Island will fall the next day. Soldiers who were able to surrender will be moved to the mainland for re-education.

President Jinping will demand that the US remain neutral, but the United States will already have begun to reinforce its Naval forces with additional Carrier Groups and relocated B-1's and B-2's. A Chinese long-range Badger that threatens and then penetrates one group's expanded zone of control is shot down by a Navy F-35C. At that point President Jinping will authorize the release of a reverse engineered Russian Rubin Design Bureau Poseidon autonomous nuclear torpedo. It will create an underwater radioactive tsunami that will roll and capsize the USS Gerald R. Ford (CVN 78) and incapacitate the entire support group. Upon detonation detection a Virginia Class Nuclear Fast Attack submarine that had been stalking a now sacrificed and newly commissioned Zhou class nuclear attack submarine that had been trailing the carrier group, fires 1 wire guided Mark 45 ASTOR. The Chinese sub is destroyed within minutes of release. Both submarines will be lost. China will not be able to confirm that her sub has gone missing for another 2 weeks.

Two Ohio Class Ballistic Missile Submarines and four additional Virgina Class Nuclear Fast Attack subs are publicized as having been pre-positioned. Beijing will threaten US forces in the region, including at Okinawa, with the deployment of the DF-27, their most sophisticated anti-ship ballistic missile, which uses a hypersonic glide vehicle to maneuver to its target. US allies including South Korea, Vietnam, Malaysia, Indonesia, Japan, and Australia will begin to deploy in the East and South China Seas. Russia will sortie from Okhotsk and Vladivostok. North Korea will threaten limited engagements which will be ignored. The Republic of China will begin to deploy M142 HIMARS as well as loitering and standoff drone munitions to counter pending amphibious operations. The war will stalemate, markets will crash, but the blockade of Taiwan will continue.

FIRE STORM 星星之火，可以燎原

1

President Jinping is setting up the trip wire that will set all of this in motion. His Taiwan Strait Joint Sword 2024B Naval Maneuver involved 90 ships that were supported by 153 aircraft, the most aggressive Chinese exercise in 3 decades. These maneuvers were designed to practice and simulate a blockade. They were initiated based on President Jinping's assumption that Trump will acquiesce.

Pentagon assessments assume that China will not achieve military superiority until 2035 at current investment levels, but this would be incorrect. President Jinping's strategy is one of regional superiority using an 'active defense' posture, an approach inspired by Mao's pronouncement that the first punch is thrown to avoid the next 100. It is a concept also based on the idea that one person should be punished to teach the next 100. Trump will be President Jinping's pupil, and President Jinping will launch his seminar on 'War as a continuation of politics' by demonstrating that the backbone of surprise is fusing speed with secrecy, an action he will initiate late in 2026 after the midterms.

President Jinping of course will be mindful of the new American President, a man he will be able to manipulate. As Mao so famously proclaimed, "We should support whatever the enemy opposes and oppose whatever the enemy supports", which will infuriate and confuse Trump because he is puerile and fatuous and makes decisions based on malice of forethought. At first Trump will refrain and even cower in response to overt military action, but because he is a weak man he is impulsive. Men will die because of it. Xi will finally comprehend that his opponent is possessed by a staggering level of aberrant narcissism motivated by dangerous incompetence – all of it backed by the world's most powerful military.

Ignorance and irrational platitudes are a key component of America's new Populist. President Jinping also is using misdirection to manipulate the Chinese Public. Ask a Xi Jinping supporter why they defer to him. Because they are so aggravatingly compliant, what you get in reply is often strangely incoherent. Why support a man who lies, manipulates their insecurities, and overtly dismisses their intelligence. That President Jinping has managed to motivate a large segment of the Chinese public implies that he possesses an insight into their fear of being abandoned by the Party. That President Jinping has risen to prominence in the Communist Party reflects a talent for manipulation more than purpose or policy. That he has weaponized his campaign using the tactics of an Autocratic Populist now means that we must ask whether he does so based on a deeply cynical view of humanity, and whether he will use a sense of entitlement to dismantle the hard-won progress China has made by re-orienting itself in favor of a more inclusive and open society.

President Jinping's supporters crave belonging but perceive that they are regarded with contempt. They are derided as being ignorant and incurious because they often are. What is unsaid is that many are submissive because they are fearful. President Jinping's supporters, embarrassed by a sense of isolation, feel that they have been rendered impotent by meritocratic standards of success, and conjure up intrigue and conspiracy as a rationale for their lot in life. They feel that treachery and collusion must be the reason why they are overlooked, and it is in this environment that President Jinping gives voice to the dis-ease they feel for facts that would otherwise convince them that they are at fault. It is in this gutter of discontent that a new Chinese Autocratic Populist finds that he can thrive.

Power accumulates and creates an overwhelming desire to maintain and protect itself. When we talk about Xi Jinping we are talking about a desire for power aggrandizement that goes back to the beginnings of all political movements inspired by a cult of personality. Inequalities exacerbated by social stratification and hierarchies do not unjustifiably deserve the blame. When allowed to blossom into hate, an appeal for radical change then breeds a desire to tear down perceived structures of exclusion and privilege. Quasi Communist Religious movements can also serve as wellsprings of hate, in that they breed intolerance and devotion to orthodoxy. Thus, Communism as a substitute for religion uses an idea of blasphemy to inculcate intolerance, which is often used opportunistically by Populists to build support.

Scapegoating by the Communist Party is not born from a desire to foment change, but rather from a need to maintain commitment. It is a motivation to maintain devotion that is then converted into power, money, and control. Communism as a Religion is the first Chinese mass marketer. The Party is China's first Influencer. One has to look no further than the quasi-political movement now represented by the military that increasingly looks more like a profit making and power aggrandizing enterprise than as a defensive arm in support of Chinese self-determination.

President Jinping has transformed the Party into a political movement that promises prosperity, but perhaps more importantly provides a sense of belonging for those who see themselves as overlooked. This movement provides vacuous absolution, an arrangement where the buyer receives certainty in exchange for their loyalty and their compliance. These congregants are susceptible to manipulation, an opportunity most often taken advantage of by a Populist or Communist Absolutist.

Although the recent Chinese experience has been one of unrestrained personal opportunity, meritocratic principles have also been used to justify wealth accumulation and a stratification of opportunity. This has unfolded into Olympian levels of wealth and social stratification in China, where social mobility can also be shown to be in decline. Hukou becomes a tool not only to control unrestrained urban growth, but also as a vehicle to maintain control over a populous clamoring for inclusion. It has already morphed from a tool to control migration into a vehicle for social control that is quickly manifesting itself as a bulwark against an erosion of Communist Party legitimacy. Unchecked it does have the power to fragment the Politburo but for now remains an indispensable tool of Party control. Done efficiently with ever more invasive surveillance mechanisms, it has the potential to convert the Communist Party into a soulless conglomerate. Managed poorly it creates the seeds of the Party's demise, as the Chinese populous refuses to back down from their demands for improved standards of living in the name of a political compliance that is married to cultural and material benefits exclusion.

Because Chinese Meritocracy, as is the case in America, has become stratified, and in many instances exclusionary, huge portions of the populous are increasingly skeptical to the idea that opportunity is an unrestricted economic precept that is available to all. This effect is growing in China, and as larger proportions of the populous participate in improved standards of living, discontent has become multi-faceted. Examples of it can be found in media, social networking, and underground political educational programs. Perhaps more importantly porous social safety nets imply that the individual is personally culpable for their level of success, which forces the less fortunate to uncomfortably conclude that security for some is procured by a reduction in benefits for others.

Zero sum politics is based on fear. A fear that one will be left behind. And when it is perceived that this is based on iniquity and a lack of fairness, that fear turns to hate. Fear opens the door to the Populist. Hate opens the door to civil disobedience.

President Jinping's program is generating increased economic instability which gives birth to tremendous personal insecurity, compounded by an absence of comprehensive social safety nets, Quasi-religious organizations move in to fill the gap. Forced underground they increase the reach of their legitimacy, further undermining the mandate currently claimed by the Communist Party. This generates a powerful desire for change which is both conservative and reactionary. When under threat this perspective will be quick to blame, and will be incapable of introspection, which otherwise would require an honest appraisal of circumstance and motivation. The focus will center on President Jinping.

A constructive evaluation of Communist legitimacy of purpose also requires an honest appraisal of motivation. For President Jinping, as for any politician, it is far easier to redirect blame to an external cause, than to question the decisions that led to failure. This is resistant to analysis and can be manipulated by half-truths that are rooted in confirmable fact, but that also abrogate the need for self-appraisal and personal responsibility. The problem for the Party is that as social stratification atrophies opportunity, ascribing challenging times to external causes becomes increasingly more challenging, and for those motivated by pride in the Chinese economic miracle this becomes impossible to reconcile.

President Jinping is a modern example of an attempt to manifest social engineering out of endemic frustration. So far this has been effective, but for Xu Jinping it has yet to manifest itself into a mass movement. We see that he is searching for this rationale in the way he cycles through platitudes and in his resurrection of Chinese communist principles of obligation to Party. For now his inability to inculcate sacrifice is due to his own aberrant narcissism, and this is what constitutes the greatest threat to his tenure as leader of the Party. If President Jinping fails, the Party will crumble around him. Consider a President Jinping who possessed a Deng Xiaoping like faith in the Chinese capacity for innovation, hard work, and an ability to manifest personal success. He would be unstoppable.

In a Meritocracy if we look at communist party oriented social welfare, we see that these programs often freeze people in place, in that they tobduce inaction and complacency. This is because these programs are half measures that frustrate rather than facilitate a productive re-integration of these populations back into the work force. Chinese dynamism is based on the idea that the individual can re-create themself but misses entirely the macro-economic pressures that put them there in the first place. Hukou and subsistence level wages only perpetuate the problem.

The obvious truth is that the disconnect that exists between free market and communist economic principles often straddle an idea of unrestrained labor markets that cannot be allowed to persist in China. This devolves into power struggles that under recognize the damage economic rebalancing causes. When mobility is prevented without programmatic social support structures, or is allowed but stymied by bureaucratic programs meant to freeze a populations in place, then from a full costing perspective this dislocation is far more expensive than a system that focuses on establishing a balance between economic inputs and outputs. What quickly becomes more apparent is that it also isolates workers, separating them from the Party, removing the sense of security it provided, no longer generating belief in the proselytizing messages of China's new Communist Populist. In this way the People become not more dependent, but instead far more independent as they strive to re-invent themselves economically.

China is re-evolving into a hereditary system that operates in a closed power loop that severs access to opportunity for people who are not part of a privileged social structure. The result is widespread frustration and dissatisfaction which are obvious harbingers of change. This will require President Jinping to look for more ways to enforce support. One way President Jinping is attempting to do this is by squeezing out disagreement and criticism at the Chinese Academy of Social Sciences (CASS), where independent thought is no longer permitted, and where employees are forced to report on colleagues who do not toe the party line. It is a presage to mediocrity in academia as 'Road Blocking Tigers' are being replaced by 'thought followers' who base research on 'elevated theory'. In this way President Jinping is attempting to exert control over the minds of the disenfranchised whom he feels must be convinced that the external world is no longer Good. President Jinping is externalizing failure and giving a voice to the idea that what was once balanced and fair has been perverted in favor of a few select nations led by the United States. In this way he uses Populism to imply that tough times were fabricated and purposefully designed to enfranchise an advantage of the few over the many.

In China optimism is now prescribed. Chinese are taught the idea of 'creative destruction' in capitalism, but for those without membership in the party this process appears uncaring, greedy, and conspiratorial. China's safety net is based on the Party, but this renders the Chinese worker vulnerable to Party restrictions on freedom of movement and controlled access to opportunity and employment. In America the safety net is easy access to credit, in Europe comprehensive government social safety nets are erected to promote social stability and ease reintegration in order to mitigate economic displacement. In China economic and social control is designed to minimize the potential for social discontent that detonate civil disruptions which challenge communist party control.

In China, as in America, those who escape economic dislocation, down deep they question the efficacy of their abilities, and fear their propensity to proactively avoid downturns. For those who have been able to maintain status and security, fortitude of purpose and the merit of justly deserved rewards is colored by an awareness that circumstance, position, and luck have played a role in their success. Their concerns regarding the precariousness of their position then motivates them to perpetuate the status quo provided by membership in the Party. In this way the desire for change, and a need to maintain a social or economic advantage springs from the same source. When this happens the groundwork is laid for an idea that manipulates both the disenfranchised and the entitled with the same message of promise provided by acquiescing to Party policy.

The Jinping acolyte does not crave change but rather craves predictability, and fears exclusion that they will not be provided with stable quality of life opportunities. This then drives them to adopt cultural frameworks that deny self-determination, and advocate for the perpetuation of bureaucracies that they perceive as being able to provide security. Interestingly this perspective does not apply to those who find their conditions the most desperate, or the most fortunate. These social outliers are too focused on continuity, either from the perspective of survival, or the maintenance of power and privilege.

Rather the spectrum that exists within the upper and lower margins of society feel like they are being buffeted by unpredictability and that they are left to fend for themselves when conditions deteriorate. They are dismayed by a realization that their position in society is subject to capricious economics, and as such they fear change. When joblessness, ill health, and social position are vulnerable to diminution, a desire for Conservatism takes hold. It is at once a desire to maintain social standing, and a motivation to refocus blame.

The disenchanted Communist has lost much more than their confidence in institutions. They have lost faith in the legitimacy of the Communist Party. They look around and see only chaos and purposelessness. Theirs is a conspiratorial outlook where favor and privilege are corrupted on an unbalanced field of injustice. The fix is in. They feel they are alone. No wonder then that they either turn to dissention, or with a sense of relief to President Jinping as an Autocratic Populist.

For the hopeless the slogans provided by President Jinping are reinterpreted as a kind of faith. Often the slogan is attached to a millennial component, and it is at this point that Xi Jinping will turn his base of support into a mass movement. It does not matter that the slogans mean nothing. In fact they require ambiguity. What they do need is a millennial component that encompasses a promised period of stability and prosperity for believers who fancy themselves the elect.

Hope can then be bred with Hate, where promises are replete with lies and a dearth of empirical evidence. Logic requires rigor. Conspiracies only require belief bolstered by a willingness to reject contradictory evidence. President Jinping's message is lazy, loquacious, and prone to anger, and because of this it is seductive. It is a technique also used by Trump, and indeed every Populist.

Communism implies a rejection of the present that presages an erosion of prerogative. This implies a continuing diminution of power that is then defined as a sign of decay. The implication is a loss of status, a zero sum perspective rooted in fear. A fear that breeds hate, sloganeering, and millennialism.

This approach to the future requires that the present be discredited. A cavalier treatment of fact and rational argument paves the way for a populist message of conspiracy that is then parroted by those who feel they have been denied opportunities for prosperity. It opens the door to ethical compromise, and a vulnerability to the manipulations of money, status and privilege. Communism married to money is filthy lucre, and it is always used to realize short terms gains by those who proffer it. Often it is used to promote ideas and policies that have no merit except for the potential for profit and power aggrandized in the hands of the few. It is an easy appeal to greed, which is also used as a short-term rationalization, but represents an irreversible compromise of Marxist-Leninist principles, creating a not inaccurate impression that the party is parasitic.

The Standing Committee of the Political Bureau of the Central Committee of the Communist Party of China, entangled in a membership process that compels them all to continuously focus on profit in order to survive, puts them on an often subtle but unavoidable path to corruption. Do not wonder that the wider Chinese public increasingly holds the Politburo in such low regard. Every party member deserves it. Their ear is bent to capitalist profiteers, not to the interest of the citizenry. They deflect criticism using the meaningless platitudes and policy arguments found in President Jinping's four volume invective on the 'Governance of China', that offers nothing of substance to the average Chinese citizen. Vacuous party principles are used to obscure all other issues.

It is in this environment that President Jinping (and also Donald Trump) as Populists find that that they can now flourish. As is needed in America, a divestiture and prohibition of all investments while in public office is needed so that a system of influence no longer takes precedence over policy. Disenfranchisement of non-party members has led to dissatisfaction. Dissatisfaction has led to dissent. Dissent leads to rebellion and the rejection of communist dogma. Money in Communist Party politics is a policy of exclusion. The Party is service, or it is profit. It cannot be both.

Investigate any business enterprise in China and you will find President Jinping's acolytes exerting influence. The force of his manipulations are everywhere, promising prosperity for loyalty. The average Chinse citizen is then often left with the impression that they have been rejected by unfair current circumstance. Party prestige has no place for this segment of the populous because they feel demeaned by a rejection of it.

Never mind that an intellectual elite considers President Jinping weak and easily manipulated. Using the language of the rural outsider President Jinping portrays himself as their champion, and in this way mobilizes the insecure citizen. In actuality he considers them expendable, while placing himself above them as the most deserving of a privileged elite.

President Jinping's electorate has evaluated itself against the American standard of success and found themselves wanting. When comparing themselves to democratic elites they find themselves always running in second place. Even those segments that have realized some measure of relative success still feel that they are on the outside looking in. These people are looking for purpose and recognition. They want to feel that they are valued and not forgotten. From some perspective it matters not from what cause they derive a sense of belonging, it only matters that they belong. Communism is an example of a meaningless collective designed to create that feeling of community. No wonder President Jinping does not disparage Mao. To do so would weaken the sense of inclusion his supporters derive from it. In effect it is a secret handshake that provides instant membership to President Jinping's collective.

The triviality of communist platitudes also offers President Jinping the opportunity to subsume the worthlessness of his own message within an irrationality of foreign conspiracy. President Jinping's supporters are then offered membership within a group that to them provides a sense of belonging where before they perceived themselves as unbearably irrelevant.

President Jinping's strategy is to re-make the international landscape by re-claiming the past and re-working the present. Indeed this has already begun with his increasingly intransigent posture toward Taiwan, his de facto annexation of the Spratlys (an annexation that shares some similarities to the Ukrainian experience, and which is not talked about enough), and his program of economic imperialism in Africa.

Countering the helplessness felt by China's populous will require more than band aid policy pronouncements by the West. President Jinping's supporters are starting to lose faith in themselves and in their perceived place as citizens of the Peoples Republic. Countering President Jinping's platitudes will require an affirmation of their place not just as citizens of China but as members of a global community. Facts matter to a Chinese citizens buffeted by meaningless Communist Party platitudes. Workers in China increasingly realize that they have a worth that goes far beyond their status as a labor resource input. Unrequited, this will gestate unease, agitation, dissent, and rebellion.

Ironically President Jinping's party member is also irredeemably arrogant. It is a shield created in the name of selfishness that also justifies anger. An anger which has within it a kernel of violent retribution against their fellow workers in the name of restoring an idea of Chinese pre-eminence on the world stage.

Communist Party members redeem the meaninglessness of their lives by telling others what to do with theirs. Access to opportunity is what is relevant to this segment of China and what they desire is a re-affirmation that they are valued, and that they belong. President Jinping manipulates this concern with fear. What he lacks is a sense of empathy regarding the affect his proposals will have on the future. For President Jinping freedom is anarchy. What he is undermining is a belief in opportunity provided ubiquitously that leverages self-realization as a feeling connected to equality. This is what is needed to unchain Chinese creativity and re-introduce the nation to the rest of the world.

The wrecking ball that Capitalist free market principles impose on the Chinese cultural experience is particularly relevant to this individual. They feel completely helpless in the face of its often harsh reconfigurations of product, process, and materials. To lend a hand to the displaced is a bedrock principle of Communism, and ideas of Comparative Advantage and free market principles are irrelevant to the insecure worker. A worker who has lost his or her income and ability to provide for his family feels lost, abandoned, and distraught. The prospect of unpaid mortgages, sub-standard housing, and lack of access to meaningful employment, further exacerbates this deep sense of dread. Protests in China have spiked in 2024, and this is because the Chinese safety net is based on privilege, which subjugates the Chinese consumer to the maddening vagaries of market overindulgence.

This is why President Jinping's message of reclamation will continue to become more strident. in fact it is necessary that he do so. What this implies is that the time to reassert integrity in International Politics has never been more important. Accommodating the President with Republican right wing 'practical' Populist and anti-democratic policies will simply embolden Xi Jinping and overlook China's citizenry. Only by inserting ourselves into a discussion of Chinese identity and culture can open, free and Democratic nations make themselves heard, and President Jinping's promise of a brave new world begin to be invalidated.

INSIPID INTEGRITY 宁为玉碎，不为瓦全

2

The modern Western mind associates Communism with Dictatorship, Dictatorship with and Fascism, and Fascism with evil. But Communism is in actuality a variation on a theme of autocratic control, and as such it is not a unique political construct, but one that has adopted the trappings of technology (propaganda) to foster control and limit entitlement. President Jinping's political program has adopted elements of Fascism and Autocracy without proclaiming itself to be so. Orban and Putin also have adopted these systemic political elements which are designed to deceive and coopt the public. From this perspective President Jinping is neither Stalinist nor Hitlerian, but rather simply an Autocrat, geared towards a racial ideal of entitlement which proposes that China was created as an anti-occidental alternative to the American ideal of Western Manifest Destiny.

A propensity for Autocracy originates in the human inclination to gravitate towards structures of mutual social support and security. The problem is that Autocracy is a construct born of the vulnerabilities inherent within federalized, democratized, or fragmented political processes. To the degree that these processes are weakened, Autocracy takes root, and eventually kills its host, the pluralistic processes that brought it into existence.

President Jinping postulates that forces are at work to coopt the Chinese Communist success story, and implies that a nefarious shifting of global entitlements has been designed to stealthily disenfranchise China through a process that aggrandizes power in the name of a corrupted world view. His adherents are not drawn to this message because it is reasonable, but rather because it allows them to belong to a group that provides access to enfranchised Party privilege. Because social mobility in China is on the decline, it does not matter precisely what this commitment involves, only that it promises access to a self-replicating social elite.

This new movement must also validate and absolve its constituents of the sense that they have failed culturally. It is absolution delivered by angry rhetoric, mirrored by their frustration. The emotion of the event is what is important, not the quality of the message. The logic of President Jinping's message is irrelevant. Unquestioning acceptance of the argument is not the issue, but rather the absorption of the tone of message. It is deceptive empathy, which is an unrecognized vulnerability that provides ample opportunity for dissent or external social influences to shine a light on Xi Jinping's declaration of common prosperity for the lie that it is.

The vulnerability of President Jinping's mass movement hides in an opportunity to convert his supporters to democratic causes. That China remains at risk from external manipulations is a message the Party ardently proselytizes. But this is a pronouncement of a Xi Jinping controlled Politburo attempting to maintain a hold on power. Holding Xi Jinping accountable from the perspective of his character and actions is part of the solution, but it is not enough. The West needs to convert this into a sacred anti-autocratic cause that reveals that the conspiracy is Jinping.

President Jinping may be ethically compromised, but his personal failings are irrelevant to his supporters. Rather by highlighting his revisionist communist ideals, or his extreme perspective on Chinese Nationalism, this will call in to question the legitimacy of what for him is an already deeply irrational appeal. It would not be enough as an example simply to say that Xi Jinping commercialized the Communist Party mandate, instead he must also be described within a framework of abuse and actions that progresses into a discussion of personal compromise. This needs to be conveyed not only as a lack of ethics, but as a travesty that is irredeemably part of his warped world view. Once done President Jinping's adherents will begin to question his suitability as Leader. One Country Under President Jinping can be used a rallying cry to refocus attention on him as a man bent on deceit.

President Jinping's movement also contains within it the seeds of internal dissent. Every movement contains within itself the potential for a new and more extreme cause, and because of this Xi Jinping will be obligated to become increasingly more extreme, which could fracture the Communist right wing. When this happens President Jinping will be compelled to supplement his message with inducements to violence.

In this way all evangelical political movements are vulnerable to extremism, which provides them a platform from which they can imagine violence in the form of fictionalized opponents. When this crystallizes into a military movement promising a purge of enemies, then an extra-national motivation to spread revolution will spring from it as an unavoidable next step in the evolution of the stridency with which China exerts its influence as a political process. It would be a revolution that is exported beyond China's borders and would foretell the dismantling of the American imperialistic hegemony. Democracy will have been rendered impotent.

Communism is a facade. There is no logical doctrine to Xi Jinping's message. Currently only slogans of meaningless tropes comprise the majority of his diatribes. He is so self-absorbed that he has no appetite to digest any subject that does not deal directly with his agenda. This is one of his great vulnerabilities, in that President Jinping has yet to manifest multi-faceted qualities that have otherwise characterized the great proselytizers of the past. His message is Nationalist, but narrow. He maintains a focus on an idea of a rejuvenated China based on historical insults, not realizing that his lack of inspiration dilutes the image China has of him. He is a Technologist, and the only message that President Jinping currently provides is an obfuscated communist ideal, not an objective program of Chinese progress. This renders him vulnerable. President Jinping has no intention of sharing his authority, but he is not China. It is the Achillies Heal of every Autocratic Populist.

When President Jinping begins to extoll the heroes and martyrs of those who adhere to him as a leader, is when he will begin to attempt the externalization of a cohesive revolutionary message, one that not only will accuse his enemies of corruption, but also require that they be countered internally. At that point he will have progressed to a stage where he will be truly dangerous for America. Proclamations of vengeance will cohere, and if he finds himself vulnerable, he will suggest even more radical proposals with which to prosecute enemies and de-stabilize opponents all in the name of saving China, actions which will in actuality be his attempt to maintain his grip on power.

To stop President Jinping, a new countervailing movement must be created. The Religious Right in America provides an unpleasant example. Mixing Religion and Politics can be a questionable tactic, but prohibitions against religion in China need to be conveyed as politicized. Moral imperatives of freedom to worship need to be used to legally to promote an unshackling of the Internet that today could be tolerably described as a straight-jacket of social control in China. Coopting these important discussions away from the Communist Party would also serve to reveal this organization as a corrupted party of money and class enmity, rather than of equality and justice.

Putin's associations with President Jinping need to be overemphasized. Provide concrete examples of how the Russian government is not to be admired but is instead an enemy of its people. Media cooption in China needs to be revealed as cronyism that focuses more on money than information. President Jinping's trope of a 'common prosperity' which he gets from Mao, needs to be revealed as the dog whistle of Autocratic Communism.

The Chinese Academy of Social Sciences (CASS) should be portrayed as a Ministry that has corrupted media in China, even beyond the precepts of Marxist orthodoxy, and that the control President Jinping exercises is done for personal gain and not for the benefit of the Nation. Gao Xiang needs to be portrayed as a Xi Toadie, and as a traitor to Communist Party ideals due to the manipulating influence of Capitalism. Demonstrate that the President has become a profit aggrandizing oligarchic capitalist working to establish a regional hierarchy of Oceania, Eurasia, and East Asia dominated by Xi Jinping himself.

These ideas are a touch conspiratorial and so somewhat problematic, but there are other alternatives for rendering the chaos President Jinping generates less intoxicating. Programs that promote ideas of social security and programmatically support concepts of self-reliance, would immediately render his message less potent. This is the reason the Politburo so adamantly resists the idea of a dissolution of Hukou. Without restricted opportunity in China the communist party member is no longer convinced that success in China is chained to party loyalty as opposed to an individual's capacity to innovate, create, and self-actualize. The tragedy for the Nation is that this contains within it the seeds of a Chinese atavistic regression back into its status as a global second-class citizen.

With youth unemployment in China hitting new highs at 19%, further exacerbated by a Male to Female gender imbalance exceeding 16%, this leaves a staggering 30 million young men without the possibility girlfriends or wives. This is China's greatest unaddressed threat which also has the potential to threaten World Peace. It does not take an inventive mind to imagine the rage this will create in unrequited young men, a frustration that will ejaculate social chaos, and eventually erupt in a crazed explosion that will spill beyond China's borders.

12 million students graduated from Chinese Universities in 2024, but youth unemployment remains intractably high. Young people in China complain that they are 'living in the garbage time of history'. Counter intuitively this Communist Party manufactured policy of social dislocation reveals the danger in dis-continuing Chinese programs of social surveillance and control. The implication is that greater surveillance is required to prevent determined gender preference in pregnancies, and to counteract the delinquency of frustrated men as they continue to take out their unrequited rage on a society that isolates them from women. It will need to be remembered that an increase of violence against Women will also be experienced and that this will require an increase in Police staffing levels, a bolstering of the judicial system, and improved mental health services, all designed to protect women in China.

Revealing any Communist hypocrisy on this policy would weaken President Jinping. There are endless examples that can be used to show how the under privileged in China have been abused by Communist policies. Describe this with a tincture of conspiracy and President Jinping's complacency on the topic will evaporate. What is the least invasive and easiest solution to the tragedy of the endemic cultural abomination of gender preference and the aborting of female fetuses? In addition to investments in crime prevention and judicial and mental health services, it is equitable and increased investments in education and family planning that empowers Women to control their own bodies and the arc of their life experience. No subversive government or neighborhood surveillance neighbor reporting on neighbor systems would then be needed.

Lastly President Jinping is not wrong when he implies that openness is one of his biggest concerns. Freedom of thought has been and will continue to enrich the Nation, and cultural diversity is easily among one of the greatest benefits of the Chinese diaspora, but unrestrained cultural alternatives now create more problems for him than it solves as he attempts to enact his program of social, economic, and cultural cohesiveness. President Jinping must necessarily control access to countervailing ideas of Party legitimacy. To him it is incomprehensible that it be done otherwise. Placing increasing strictures on the free flow of information will not cause China to reject President Jinping. It contains no immediate policy risk for him, but will plant the seeds that lead to his removal as the Paramount Leader of the Party.

For generations now Chinese citizens have been forced into a mode of survival because of Party cruelty. In spite of the Nation's single party structure this has generated an atomistic political relationship with the Party that has by necessity fostered self-reliance. These self-engineered Chinese citizens are the least receptive to President Jinping's message. That this is beginning to change only indicates that prior economic challenges are ending, which ironically provides an exploitable opportunity for Jinping.

China is on the cusp of a new wave of prosperity, but President Jinping appears to be making an investment in foreign policy intransigence. It is a program based on Chinese Communist Dogma and as such it is myopic, narrow minded, and will cause dismay in a China that is now aware of the potential, profit, and promise offered by a welcoming acceptance of the Chinese cultural experience into the world community.

President Jinping's diatribes have a distinct flavor of the disingenuous. Does the man actually believe what he is saying? We wonder if his obvious meaningless platitudes are simply the rantings of an individual lacking in any ethical or moral guard rails or whether it is the product of unrestrained self-interest. Indeed the stridency of his self-absorption does appear to take on characteristics of extreme narcissism and addiction to power. Whatever the cause, perhaps encompassing elements of all of the above, the human capacity for rationalization is unbounded in a mind is willfully constrained by Marxist-Leninism. It is the dogmatic foundation of his message that gestates in the worst elements of his base.

There was a calculated motivation for his remarks that that China must adopt a "One Country, One People, One Ideology, One Party, and One Leader" political perspective in order to solidify his view of China's relationship vis a vis the US. This perspective is preparing China for the very real possibility of a policy designed to achieve results via violence of action, as exhibited in the pronouncement that "the complexity and difficulty of the national security issues we now face have increased significantly. ...We must adhere to bottom-line and worst-case-scenario (perspectives), and get ready to undergo the major tests of high winds and rough waves, and even perilous, stormy seas".

President Jinping's conscious and uncompromising approach to re-claiming a historical territorial legacy is two pronged. It asserts Chinese Nationalism while refocusing attention away from internally destabilizing cultural rejections of an opulent Party lifestyle. It is an abject rejection of the 2019 statement he made when he said that "If countries retreat to secluded islands, human civilization will die out because of a lack of exchanges." A truism that he now puts at risk for all of China because he feels China has or will soon achieve military and economic parity with the US. Interestingly this retrenchment also contains within it the seeds of his own dissolution. Indeed it has already begun.

Foreign investment is beginning to retrench, 2 in 5 marriages now end in divorce, and internally cracks are beginning to be seen in civic disruptions as exhibited by 'revenge on society' canary in the coal mine urban disturbances as exhibited in the 5 mass attacks and the murder of 53 along with an injury of elementary students the occurred in the 6 weeks since September. Police cars have begun to be stationed at schools and nurseries. It would be interesting to know if these attacks were initiated by unemployed single men, a cultural affect also experienced in the US. This is a new and unexpected manifestation of Chinese discontent that will continue to grow. Unchecked it will result in widespread and aggressive anti-government demonstrations that will turn violent.

The mistake of Tiananmen was that China now knows that demonstrations against authority cannot be conducted without the risk of injury or death. Any spontaneous demonstration against the Party will by default prompt an aggressive response by a government that will be prepared to counter protests with violence. This will incline dissenters to prepare an equally aggressive reaction, which is a prelude to civil war. Atomized individual aggression will consolidate and devolve into endemic guerilla like sometimes coordinated attacks that will continue to spiral as the government responds with increasing levels of violence. At that point President Jinping's legitimacy will evaporate and the process will begin to remove him from power.

President Jinping's view of the world is unconsciously biased and is a subject worthy of investigation. The fact remains Xi Jinping's world view is abjectly racist, and prone to stereotyping to the point where a rejection of diversity takes on a mantle of fascism. In this way Xi Jinping appeals to the most decrepit elements of his base in a way that influences and radicalizes his entire platform. His detractors may publicly deride his inability to be more thoughtful about the needs of the average Chinese citizen, but in fact his aberrance and anger that China is still considered a second-class world citizen that underscores and validates his festering frustrations. Inevitably he will reconcile this disconnect in an attack on Taiwan. It will happen. And if Trump exhibits a willingness to apply realpolitik in his relations with Xi Jinping it will happen before Trump leaves office.

Trump is like the woodsman (班门弄斧) showing off his skills before a Master Carpenter. Trump is an ignorant and embarrassing neophyte, and will be taken to the Woodshed by President Jinping, who will achieve short-term military and diplomatic success, but at the expense of China being further cut off from the rest of the world. This will accomplish the goal of ending the Taiwanese regime, but interestingly will also likely result in Xi's removal from office, and a third and successful impeachment of Donald J. Trump, whose post term successor will be less pliant when it comes to accommodating dictators

The Communist intent is not to integrate globally but to dominate. What we will experience is a national discourse that is conducted at the extremes of the political spectrum. Compromised Communist influencers and academics will be given free rein to proselytize xenophobia which will vie for acceptance among the worst of Chinese political society, and encompass conspirators, political profiteers, racists, opportunists, and yes even foreign national media infiltrators, who will be targeted by President Jinping to raise the vilest of emotions and inculcate an appeal to weakest among his political base. Counter arguments will then be rendered ineffectual because the appeal is based on emotion not fact. This will lead not to respectful debate but the forceful prevention of dissent further isolating President Jinping from the rest of China.

Disputes with President Jinping need to be configured as logical refutations that attempt to parse his lies with fact, but that also supplants refutation with a strident and even exaggerated counter warning that brings forth its own emotional obligation. Done correctly his fringe fence sitting supporters will be induced to convert to a new imperative based on Deng Xiaoping's evaluation of a future where China re-engages with the World. The danger here of course is that all perspectives are compromised, which then opens the door to incredulity on both sides.

Redemption for the unredeemed who consider themselves irredeemable in China requires that President Jinping configure a message that leverages tropes and platitudes that are impervious to structured analysis. These statements will need to offer their recipients a way to lose themselves in a debate that is resistant to introspection. This is why President Jinping's (and Trump's) base remains static, and also why it appears to be eclectic, encompassing racial, nihilistic, isolationist, and racist segments of the body politic. China is increasingly vocal about its anti-Japanese sentiments, from some perspectives not unjustifiably, which has recently manifested itself in attacks against Japanese expatriates.

That Japan does not acknowledge its historical crimes, starting with Nanjing, is incomprehensible. Of course this also applies to the United States, and the historical imperialism of any nation, all of whom still need to take responsibility for their transgressions against humanity. To paraphrase Balzac, great wealth always begins with a crime. For the US this was achieved not with one crime, but with two - the disgrace of Slavery and the Genocide of the Plains Indians.

For Britain it is the same, the disgrace of Imperialism in China and India, and indeed the World. Every nation has amends to make. Consider the impact of diplomatic appeasements based on an acknowledgement of the disgrace of Imperialism, starting with Japan, Britain, and the United States, that acknowledges the racist domination and diminution of what was a glorious Chinese historical and cultural identity. Its impact could re-start reconciliation and by itself re-open China to world. The entire world would breathe a sigh of relief. Sadly, President Jinping is willing to pervert this frustration to sacrifice an increasingly versatile Chinese modern cultural experience in pursuit of his goal of Chinese retribution.

DIALECTIC DISSOLUTION 蚁穴溃堤

3

The average Chinese citizen is aware that they lack a voice, but they still possess a will to dissent. Providing the Chinese public small vehicles that offer anonymous political expression has the potential to generate significantly improved outcomes in Chinese perspectives about their relationship to their nation and the rest of the World. This will create within them an awareness of the possibility of a reversal of current fortunes with recognizable avenues to realize improved standards of living. Their current lack of a safety net, and a systemic awareness that their concerns are not recognized as a priority by the Communist Party, provides them with the rationale for a wholesale rejection of the current order.

The People's Party becomes an agent of chaos which is used as a means to inculcate a supposed manifest contract with past policies of openness. The Party then is perceived as hypocritically orienting itself towards an aggrandizement of power in the name of obligations to orthodoxy as an excuse to be exclusionary. The class of Chinese citizen it directs its appeal to already considers themselves rudderless without party membership. This is why President Jinping's trope of "The Chinese people are a great people; they are industrious and brave, and they never pause in pursuit of progress" rings as an empty promise to those who are on the outside looking in.

Economic uncertainty creates anxiety and fear, which then swells the ranks of President Jinping's detractors. The economic reality of low-income wage earners is far different than the macroeconomic imperatives dictated by a Communist Party Five-Year Plan for Social Development, which rebalances labor inputs without consideration for those who are left adrift financially. This is a ready catalyst for frustration and dissatisfaction for millions of Chinese. Here again we see the failings of a Communist system that perverts capitalist principles and which swells the ranks of President Jinping as Populist. Ironically, it is in a Populists' interest to continue these dislocations even while offering vacuous solutions regarding the same, which is why the educational system is left broken by the Communist party. It is in their interest to leave it injurious in the name of imposing restraints on the population in the name of social control. This perpetuates alienation and fosters civil disobedience in the name of Patriotism, which can then be externalized by President Jinping in support of Chinese patriotism.

Those who are hopelessly and intractably poor on the other hand are isolated from the vicissitudes of economic cycles. They neither benefit from nor participate in the transitory benefits offered by the ebb and flow of Socialist Communism. Rather it is the unemployed who internalize loss and develop unfocused anger. They once possessed a right to the benefits provided by the Deng Xiaoping program of openness and opportunity, but are now left adrift and unacknowledged, all while those who control access to capital via Party membership reorient in favor of more profitable relationships with the economy

Trickledown economics, an idea developed in America, is nothing more than an enfranchisement of privilege, a caricature of economics that says I will give you a little, and that means more for me. President Jinping has said that "Some foreigners with full bellies have nothing better to do than engage in finger-pointing at us. First, China does not export revolution; second, it does not export famine and poverty; and third, it does not mess around with you. So what else is there to say?" What else is left is that just as Putin established a new Oligarchic aristocracy, and as America has used the excuse of Meritocracy to rationalize stratospheric accumulations of wealth in the hands of the .01%, so too has President Jinping created a new Chinese Nobility, a Communist Party Bourgeoisie that is nothing more than a blatant attempt to maintain privilege and continued access to power.

In all three Nations the base has swelled and become increasingly frustrated. All three countries will eventually implode as this collapses in a rejection of class stratification. Indeed America has already begun to do this in its fascist move towards Trump. Unfortunately this increases the danger of conflict for China, and commensurately constitutes a blow back of increased risk for the US. What will be used to temporarily stop the rot will be foreign war entanglements that obliquely reference one nation versus the other, but even these defocusing exercises will weaken each regime and cause their political structures to de-legitimize. We see a ready-made example of this in Putin's attempt to defocus the Russian population away from the failings of his government. In so doing Putin has sown the seeds of his own removal. President Jinping and President Trump will experience the same.

Capitalism still has role to play in economic strategy in China, but it must be acknowledged that unrestrained free markets while efficient are inherently inhumane. Recognizing this plight, without denouncing the necessity for resource and capital allocation requirements, will give a voice back to at risk workers if they are offered alternatives to the One China promise. Recognition and support will provide them with a willingness to work within the system, as opposed to overtly rejecting it in favor of temporary but unpredictable change. Otherwise, the dynamism of China will be squandered by rising frustration which will search for a place to direct blame and appease anger at unfulfilled quality of life improvement promises.

Consider the Chinese worker displaced by the concept of Comparative Advantage, a worker who has had his job ripped from him by Trump imposed tariffs and an inexplicable Xi Jinping mandated isolationism, never mind the dangers of disinflation. That this worker might now have his job ripped from him once again in the name of a resurgent America would feel anti-communist to him.

The Politburo, by allowing Communist dogma to cherry pick definitions of what Capitalism means is one of the great weaknesses of the Xi Jinping message. Instead it should acknowledged that Capitalism is efficient but uncaring, that free market principles need to be 'socialized', and that people as opposed to profits need to come first. Interestingly America would benefit from this perspective as well. This idea could be considered the midpoint of a compromise between Communism on the Left, and Capitalism on the Right. President Jinping may imply this, and Trump my prevaricate to it, but clearly profits are more important to both of them, which necessitates the reallocation of capital at the expense of each their citizenry.

While not acceptable according to Communist Dogma, this process does generate growth, although the lion's share of the benefit does accrue to the wealthy. Economic stability is abrogated in favor of the efficiencies achieved via economic dislocation. In Capitalist terms 'the creative destruction' of productive capability. Speaking this obvious fact to the Nation has already been silenced by Chinese media, which has given power to the creative lie now parroted by President Jinping's Communist Party.

For the common worker the fear of losing something is always felt more keenly than the hope of gaining it. An employee who understands that his position is tenuous has the not incorrect impression that his disadvantage provides others benefit. The idea is that the fix is in, and the loser is him. This becomes an intolerable idea that quickly leads to hate, which can easily foster violence.

President Jinping will target this segment of the populous, not in terms of the small proportion of citizens who have yet to vocalize discontent, but instead as a reassessment of this entire class segment as posing a danger to the stability of the Party. He will use their vulnerability to stoke a Populism designed to maintain the People's hypnotized belief in a Communist Party unreality.

President Jinping's doctrine is fluid but impervious to revision. Like Trump, his message funnels the focus onto his policy as a brand, and it is in this that he remains vulnerable. The idea of President Jinping has yet to coalesce around the concept of Xi Jinping as Savior, that his Presidency was preordained – something he has already indirectly proffered. This though also has within it the potential to turn him into a joke and would render him vulnerable. In America Trump is considered to be a clown for just this reason. President Jinping's robotic countenance, his monotone, dry and anti-climactic elocution, reveals him to be uninspired and incurious. President Jinping is dreary and monotonously vainglorious. It is an unleveraged opportunity that must be utilized by detractors who desire a return to Deng Xiaoping's campaign of rapprochement with the West.

President Jinping and his acolytes talk about Party loyalty, but in fact it is these aspects of surrender that cause the anxiety experienced by his supporters. Freedom to take the initiative places the burden of success on the individual. This is broken when planning mandates market dynamics. A winner takes all competition then occurs internal to the Party, not within the dynamics of the marketplace, which is then accompanied by endemic corruption as competition grows beyond the stricture of ethical propriety.

For President Jinping's followers freedom is a burden. They will gladly relinquish it for status and security. This renunciation of choice is what President Jinping craves. He uses it to aggrandize power in his pursuit of personal glorification, and in the process he irredeemably damages the promise of openness and that was used to create the economic miracle that is the China of today.

What workers in the China now see is a system that sacrifices their stability and security in favor of a process that distributes benefits among an entitled few. They see a Politburo prepared to lend an ear to monied interests as opposed to the Citizenry. This is why President Jinping's supporters have begun to question Communist legitimacy. Xi Jinping has not transformed the Communist Party but rather absorbed it. Deng Xiaoping policy strategists who wish to regain influence must recognize the practical concerns of the People while creating a narrative of Xi Jinping as a Populist and con artist who lacks any concern for the common worker.

This is why President Jinping continues to preoccupy himself with loyalty in order to repel opponents, both internal and external. Freedom of initiative is reshaped into a sacrifice of the Proletariat. In this way he removes any opportunity for dissent. Ironically, it is this surrender of individualized action that offers his adherents their sense of having escaped their own shortcomings and failures.

President Jinping's supporters crave a need to be lost in the movement. Alone they is vulnerable, as part of a group they are immune from the demoralizing insecurity of being ruthlessly assessed and reassessed in terms of their behavior at home, and their performance on the job. They crave an escape from the incessant battle to stay one step ahead of one's peers.

Gradually President Jinping is converting his message from one of obligation, to a doctrine that promises the fruits of a system that rejects classical communism as not being capable of providing the benefits that can be realized by a re-organized China. President Jinping's supporters in this way do not crave freedom of action but rather equality within a Xi Jinping re-defined system of benefits and justice.

President Jinping's tax structure has all of China paying for his vanity projects including his road and belt project. Never mind that as he turns the nation inward the return on this investment will turn negative. His Party is complicit in this in that they are poised to derive significant profits from the effort. They will prosper. The Nation will suffer. The Politburo is complicit both directly and indirectly in promoting funding that perpetuates this iniquity. The Communist Party, as is the case for the American Congress, has been corrupted by money. Meaningful reform and a restoration of faith in its institutions will not be possible until wide ranging changes are applied to the process of capital allocation that transparently promotes social stability and opportunities for all Chinese.

Under President Jinping the citizenry feels isolated and attacked by the system. Education provides a particularly poignant example, where the wealthy are provided with endless avenues from which to capture opportunities generationally. This is no different than the corrupted meritocratic system experienced in America. Harvard has been reviled as a singularly corrupt example via the hypocrisy of its 'legacy based' admissions process. A process that has shown itself to be captured by money, power, and a sense of entitlement. It is so fraught with abuse that it has become the single greatest cause for disparaging the elite in America. Donald Trump is a product of this system. An incurious man who does not read and bases his decisions on media favorability ratings. He is the product of Wharton that uses an admissions process that often prioritizes wealth above ability. America and China both suffer from this distorted process of promotion. That such warped men could rise to a position of prominence speaks to a broken educational system in America and in China.

President Jinping and President Trump are examples of a process of political distillation where the dangerous foreshot is allowed to remain in the Political Soup. They may initially inebriate the electorate but eventually they kill the Host.

Like Trump, President Jinping is an example of political hubris. President Jinping continually trumpets economic exhortations for Chinese economic exceptionalism. This is purposeful misdirection, intended to divert attention away from the fact that his programs benefit the largest 1% of Communist Party members. What must be done is to highlight this camouflage by providing examples of Chinese excess as was done by Russian ex-patriot dissenters who reported about Putin's Palace in Sochi. Show where Xi Jinping's programs have failed, and highlight the misuse of Party wealth, including their planes, their homes, and other luxury acquisitions that perpetuate rather than resolve the plight of the average Chinese citizen. The outrage would grow, and his support would wane.

Money in China invalidates the voice of those who do not have it. Highlight this and demonstrate how President Jinping, regional governors, and Chinese Conglomerates use money to manipulate political policy. Reveal Xi Jinping and his Communist Party for the frauds they are. Public Service is not for profit. No wonder the forgotten Chinese citizen rejects President Jinping and his communist party old guard. Every member is to some degree complicit.

The free flow of information is under assault in China, and increasing strictures can be anticipated. Communist party reformations will stagnate unless transparency is enabled with opportunities to provide critical feedback on policy and bureaucratic processes. External sources of information must be provided that demonstrate that

President Jinping is an outsider, and deeply embedded in this system of abuse. Exposing him to be an adept manipulator of a political process entrenched in corrupting quid pro quo will go a long way in exposing him to be as much of a fraud as Trump is.

President Jinping's favorability ratings in China are ambiguous, meaning the average Citizen in China is lukewarm to his leadership. Among the Diaspora it sits at 35%. Given that Party participation has a current de-facto limit of around 7% President Jinping is confronted with shaking lose the apathy the nation has for Marxist-Leninism. There is a reason Communism failed in the USSR. Marxism is based on a fiction that changes endlessly to fit the needs of the those in power. It is an obvious fallacy that can only be secured by conjuring up propaganda. The easiest way this will be accomplished is with continued aggressive posturing against Taiwan. The danger here is that this becomes a self-fulfilling prophesy, where military conflict with the West is inevitable, something that appears not entirely undesirable from President Jinping's perspective based on his current rhetoric.

But all of this misses the bigger picture. If he is successful, it will herald a retrenchment of the economic and cultural Chinese miracle and imply the successful implementation of a pervasive and all-invasive nationwide surveillance society bolstered by AI. It would presage a new and dangerous era for humanity that will have experienced a world-wide genesis in a Xi Jinping program of fanatic Nationalism consolidated by Chinese Communist Autocracy.

Target the 93% of the Chinese populous who do not partake in the benefits of Party membership. Induce them to compare their living standards with a wider and far more open global economic and cultural framework. This will require revealing to the individual that they are discredited by the Party, a disconnect that can be represented by diminished standards of living. It does not matter that Chinese poverty has been dramatically reduced. No one looks at where they came from when assessing status. We all only look at where we want to be in order to get what we don't have. Magnified, this unrequited want transforms into civil discontent, discontent into civil disobedience, and disobedience into civil war. Attempts in the past have been made to highlight President Jinping's hypocrisy in this area. It should be done so again. Show where he and his major contributors continue to outsource discontent in order to accumulate money and power.

Burgeoning doubts about President Jinping will begin to disengage the Chinese Proletariat. Supplement this with Socialist proposals that would level the playing field between rural and urban China. This would propose support structures that equalize the benefits provided to rural citizens. Place the focus on the lost productivity and earning potential of the Chinese worker. This will generate an awareness of unfairness in employment, and by stating that these practices are used to restrain workers in order to direct opportunities to others, this would immediately render President Jinping's proposals less appealing. Done effectively it will create anger and divisiveness among his ranks.

The far right Communist, unintentionally it seems, is utilizing a two-pronged approach in creating rage to generate acquiescence to policy. On the one hand they highlight cultural decay, and on the other relentlessly attack democratic (American) institutions as unfair. When one considers that the male birth rate in China remains unsustainably high from a social stability perspective, an evaluation of cultural mores is not without merit.

When this is also considered from the compounding problem of unemployment, more specifically youth unemployment, then you have a potent motivator for rejecting communist processes and policies. Law and Order is reinterpreted by an Autocratic Populist to imply that greater control is needed over political processes in order to restore stability to cultural and social institutions. But when shown in the light of the opportunities that are available outside of China, what occurs is an irresistible thirst for information that is not controlled by the Communist Party.

Economic dislocation also breaks family bonds, an important aspect of Chinese cultural life. Although the Party emphasizes the need for stability in family structure, communist principles of sacrifice contradict this call for devotion to community. Communist policies actually exacerbate the disconnect, which offers the Populist an opportunity to proselytize a message that engenders fanaticism and hatred. Hatred that inevitably leads to violence. Economic dislocation is a necessary prerequisite to Populism and to President Jinping's approach to policy in that it provides him the rationale for proposing processes that enlarge the scope of social control.

Comparisons that highlight disparities in extra-national economic opportunity and investments in social infrastructure, are what will stimulate discussions about President Jinping's promise of progress. If this had pre-existed in an accessible and meaningful way in China, President Jinping would never have evolved to the position of influence he currently enjoys. There is a reason why Xi Jinping never talks about concrete and immediate proposals for improving education, unemployment compensation, and equitable health care. It contributes unproductively to his program of divisiveness and manipulation.

The Chinese political system preaches, it does not teach. Western sources must teach, not preach, and provide examples of support structures that promote self-reliance, all within an inclusive system that promotes the value of the individual. Hope needs to replace helplessness. Currently Chinese social safety nets do nothing but sequester the recipient, thereby providing President Jinping ready subscribers for his program of international retrenchment.

President Jinping's supporters are desperate to escape the meaninglessness of their participation in the Chinese political process. The burden of citizenship for them has been transformed into personal sacrifice. The West needs to offer them the opportunity to rejoin the global community both economically and culturally. Ultimately the benefit will accrue to us all - in a diminution of Chinese popularism, and in an increased propagation of extra-national Chinese expatriate critiques of Xi. To counter President Jinping it needs to be shown that his aim is to continue the sacrifice of the forgotten Chinese Proletariat in order to benefit a new Chinese Communist Bourgeois Aristocracy, and that his program is an illusion designed only to help him maintain and aggrandize power.

President Jinping's doctrine fosters enmity, not only against his enemies but also within its own ranks, as his acolytes use flattery to vie for approval and approbation. One only needs to look so far as to the feuds that already exist within the communist party and the propagandistic pranks perpetuated by the Chinese Academy of Social Sciences (CASS).

What we see is that the Xi Jinping acolyte is apprehensive, distrustful, skeptical, and vacuous. Their purpose lacks definition, and in this way they grasp for accolades and approval from the one person who cares for their input the least. This creates within them an obedience, but one that is adopted without a sense of shame. This division shows how President Jinping maintains control over the Communist Party. It is geared to focus support not on principle but on the President. It is wasteful and vulnerable in that this expenditure of internal resources of control weakens the Party. Everything Xi Jinping touches is camouflage. Resurrect principles of Socialism freed from the restraint of Marxism and Leninism, in the spirit of democratic inclusiveness and a rejuvenation of Deng Xiaoping's program of the Four Modernizations. President Jinping's doctrine of deception and power aggrandizement will then be revealed to be singularly focused on the man himself to the determent of the entire nation.

COMRADES AND CAPITALISM

道之以政，齐之以刑，民免而无耻；道之以德，齐之以礼，有耻且格

4

If you teach a child to hate, they will eventually learn to disrespect their teacher. 30 to 55 million people died during the Great Leap Forward, much of it caused by local Communist party cadres who exacerbated the situation via controls on food distribution. A policy disturbingly similar to one used by Stalin that would lead to the crime and tragedy of the Ukrainian Holodomor. The ranks of Chinese scholarship would also be decimated during this period. Communist principles have been used to justify crimes in the past and they are being used to do so again.

Communism espouses a shared purpose of national progress, but is now attempting to overlay this with a communal approach to Capitalism. This has turned Communism into a perversion of principles, and even an abandonment of the precepts of Capitalism. President Jinping's program is neither communist nor capitalist. All it does is aggrandize Profit in the hands of a few. Instead what must be done is to show that a western approach to capitalism distributes benefits more widely by prioritizing the needs of the marketplace. This is what must be communicated in order to create a bulwark against President Jinping's program of retrenchment. It is marketplace and banking reform, fairness in social services, supportive workers compensation, and retraining that does not isolate the worker, along with radically reformed personal bankruptcy laws, long term and fully funded mental health and addiction recovery programs, and a reformed criminal justice system that does not prosecute for heresy against doctrine. This is what President Jinping will never implement, and what is needed as informational feedback generated by the world's democracies to re-orient perspectives about government in China.

Capitalism fosters a reorientation of inputs, and when that input is Labor this creates magnified levels of insecurity generating waves of psychological distress. Obviously, this is a field ripe for demagogy. President Jinping's program is intended to magnify the weaknesses of this system. In other words, to leverage the dislocation of free markets, and incline those affected to reject it, all while deriding the process as anti-communist. It matters not how irrational and contradictory this is, only that it gives voice to dislocation in favor of autocratic control.

It is the opposite of a system designed to foster and support self-reliance. Xi Jinping does this in the name of consolidating power. Taken to an extreme as it is with hukou, it creates inequality and is inherently destabilizing. The total cost of fully burdened production must be considered when evaluating economic benefits, including those costs related to job destruction and intra-national migrations – both physical, mental, and political. When these costs are comprehensively addressed in terms of their impact on crime and mental health, President Jinping will have come a long way in objectively applying humanistic perspectives to the principles of capitalism.

Last and not least China needs to become a nation that emphasizes education over defense. How would Xi Jinping pay for it? He already does, many times over, in lower productivity, higher crime, and more expensive health care. Consider the affect. Open door Communism is not denied but strengthened. The body politic is transformed into a source of pride via a humble recognition that every individual is valuable even while emphasizing one nation and one people. In this way the Republic is transformed into a cohesive whole invulnerable to the disease of Autocratic Communist Populism. President Jinping and future populist communist pretenders would be revealed as weak, meaningless, irrelevant, and impotent.

Another area of weakness that must be confronted is in an idea of a China that provides self-actualization for those enlightened enough to leverage the possibilities offered by Marxist-Leninism. The internet wealth creation engine, and now the promise of riches offered by investments in the military, along with investments in infrastructure and energy generation, only serve to confuse and isolate many Chinese from the promise of the Chinese Communist economic miracle. When this is combined with extreme wealth accumulation as exemplified by Chinese millionaires who invest in 6 million dollar duct taped bananas that parade as bourgeoisie examples of Art, this creates an inevitable distrust in President Jinping's government, which is then reflected in dissatisfaction that leads to disengagement.

For supporters of the Deng Xiaoping policy of global engagement, shared purpose should not be promoted as a focus on the Communist Party, but rather at the level of the body politic. Not as a decision subsuming the individual to a national imperative, but instead as a vehicle from which an individual can feel themself as being part of the ongoing Chinese tradition of innovation. The Party, while cohesive, ideally would be rendered unnecessary in that improved standards of living, social safety nets and improved universal health care would allow the Chinese corporate firmament to reorganize without relying on government subsidies.

The Party has shown itself to be vulnerable to internal abuse and is an inefficient waste of resources. Livable wages and comprehensive social safety nets that help rather than hinder employment flexibility are what is needed. Consider the Chinese Corporation freed from the cost of adhering to Chinese dogma, and the egregious waste of subsidized production quotas and competition constrained marketplaces. The benefits would far outweigh the burden.

China needs concrete proposals that unambiguously implement open access to information and education. A proposal for the same external to the communist controlled media network would immediately convey a recognition of this fact. Investigations that confirm the need for increased investments in social programs, could then be configured as open source and not tied to Party privilege. In this way every person and business could be portrayed benefiting from an economy that exists on a level playing field. Everyone would participate to the same degree regardless of relationship to Party – a bedrock principle of Communism.

Any arrangement of employees and support systems should include and also benefit the employer. Nothing prevents a programmatic approach to Capitalism from incorporating support structures and stable transition alternatives for the corporation as well. Just not from the perspective of a Communist Party economic referee who fixes the game because they have been paid to do so. Productive capability should not be isolated from competition, but rather supported with mechanisms that level the competitive playing field both domestically and internationally, and provide support for integrated programs that foster cost of labor efficiencies – China's greatest comparative advantage.

Tempered Capitalism is a way to free the worker from the cruelties of an impersonal economic system that leaves workers stranded. If this is couched in the lexicon of an enlightened communism so be it. Bureaucracy disengaged from political bias, organized to be impartial, must absorb the economic transient in a way that reprioritizes their reincorporation back into the economic framework. It needs to be remembered that an accumulation of wealth in the hands of a few is accompanied by burgeoning social stratification and de-humanizing Shehui Guhua , and that this is inherently destabilizing. It is as if the weight of this structure becomes unsupportable at its base and eventually collapses in upon itself in an implosion of populist misinformation, xenophobia and militarism. President Jinping's solution will be the bane of China and the World, and will be aggressively countered by the US.

Today the message of the Chinese Communist Party defies deconstruction, purposefully. It is not truth and is intentionally mutable. Any attempt to rationalize it becomes a futile attempt to expose the irrelevance of the message, because the message does not endeavor to establish a factual framework, but rather is an invitation to participate in a manic community of make believe – believers who then become impervious to argument unless provided with a new ideological community within which they can express elation in membership.

President Jinping's appeal to the pseudo religious communist is also blatantly hypocritical. Already China is Communist in name only. Today it adopts the hall marks of Capitalism converted into despotism by fiat. Pseudo religious communists overlook a so obviously corrupted man because his appeal is not to his ethics or even his proselytizing message, but is instead to his pronouncements of strength and his declaration that he can overcome unenlightened and inept institutions – a campaign tactic that is also used by Donald Trump. This is what has generated the new and burgeoning creation of a politicized Communist Bourgeoisie that preaches warped Leninist doctrines of Chinese cultural superiority and Manifest Destiny. History is rife with examples of intransigent religious movements. American far right Christian Nationalists also take advantage of the same in order to increase influence and generate access to power, and in this way they are no different than Chinese Communists working to generate influence. All the better that President Jinping's message reinforces orthodoxy. It is cynical but profitable – a cynicism that works on both sides of the Pacific.

The modern Chinese Communist has become in some ways sequestered and scorned, and this has only served to reinforce their sense of isolation vis a vis a wider China. It has also created the catalyst for their belief in President Jinping. Coastal Chinese politics, a geographic demography replicated in the US, describes rural populations as ignorant and easily misled. Party loyalty, and devotion to family and ancestral cultural connections, seem irretrievably contradictory, but to the far right communist these ideas are the same, in that command and control over self and country is needed to protect the sanctity of the citizen and the Party. The scorn levied on them by a more enlightened and educated Chinese elite is what creates in them the uneasy conviction that President Jinping's program is an avoidable necessity in their fight to actualize a moral China which respects Communist tradition. On the other hand for the Xi Jinping acolyte he offers them a welcoming incorporation of privilege and opportunity, militaristic pride and purpose, country and corporation, all in one far right megalith of Party and Country.

What increases the danger posed by President Jinping is his appeal as a mass movement Populist and as a leader of the military. Armies are by default compact, cohesive, and hierarchical. Ideals of glory are often conveyed to the soldier in religious imagery. The soldier does not need to grant his allegiance to a populist, he only needs to be told that it is so. Loyalty, camaraderie, and a violent action of purpose are what predominate in a soldier's mandate. The soldier has long ago reconciled himself to a loss of autonomy and accepted that his allegiance is not to him alone. It only matters that he belongs. The brotherhood he experiences swells significantly when supplemented with semi-religious pollical orthodoxy, much less messianic legitimacy.

A more targeted reflection on the motivations that are manipulated by President Jinping need to narrow a consideration of circumstance. Unexpected dissention that continues to percolate throughout China creates anxiety for President Jinping's government, but might reassure Western democracies that his political appeal is waning. This would be premature. Current dissent is a presage that discontent is growing, and some cultural divisions, especially those of the youth segment, and of young men in particular, appear to be trending towards anarchy, but intractability in these numbers would be misleading. Youth are as a condition of their stage in life inherently restless. If Xi Jinping offers them opportunities to realize independence, they will quickly transition themselves.

A mandate to enable just such a state is complicated in that it is constrained by the Male to Female ratio imbalance in China, perhaps President Jinping's largest potential source of social chaos. It is an impending social earthquake that may only be rectified by War. Perhaps by unleashing the 16% of Chinese men without women against the 8% of Indian men without the same. Barring the efficacy of such a solution, this can be more realistically rectified by increasing social control. Abortion of female fetuses must also be strictly outlawed along with prohibitions against the Bride Price tradition. The problem here for President Jinping is that accelerated programs of social control will exacerbate dissention, further isolating disenfranchised Chinese. China has had enough. Its citizens do not want to live in an 'information cocoon'. This an the opportunity for

Westen Media, in that un-balanced reproduction dynamics underscore a system where Communist policies de-stabilize that most basic of human instincts. Only an excessive amount of social control will overcome the chaos, heralding the start of an era of where the government wages war against her own , and where thought police become a resurrected but a now all powerful renunciation of the Four Olds - old customs, culture, habits, and ideas. This will be the beginning of the end for China. It will constitute a great leap backward from which the Communist Party will never recover.

This then implies that the welcoming promise of higher education opportunities available in the United States could serve to invalidate the Gaokao and the Civil Service Exam. This would confirm that Shehui Guhua and Hukou is a manufactured part of a process designed not to impose fairness and social stability but is instead designed to perpetuate privilege. The implication is that this will become a permanent part of a Chinese system of social stratification that can only be ended with a dissolution of the Xi Jinping regime.

Interestingly the United States is also grappling with this idea that social mobility has been invalidated through restrictions in fair access to educational opportunity. In the US it has transformed into a perversion of the idea of Meritocracy that that has already manifested itself in a political move to the Republican right that incorporates the idea that an Imperial Presidency is needed to change the system. America also is paying the price for under-investments in education. The result, a singularly incurious, ignorant, and unqualified President who will embarrass the Nation, dismay the World, and threaten China with his racist perspectives on the Orient. Both nations will find that they are at a crossroads, in that reformation will put them on a path to fairness and justice, or that transformation will foster an aggrandizement of power, where privilege and prosperity are stratified in order to maintain zero sum control over other more reactionary portions of the populous. China will be leashed and impoverished, and America stripped of her capacity for creative economic flexibility. There are ample historical precedents for this. The alternative is a world where every nation benefits from Chinese dynamism and America's willingness to embrace diversity. The whole world would profit, but none more so than China itself.

This is the great fallacy of President Jinping's program of Chinese Nationalism. It is a lie based on an idea of Nationalistic Pride, that in actuality is designed to solidify the idea President Jinping as a Great Leader. Carried to fruition it demeans the entire Chinese populous. President Jinping is not the Nation, he is its steward, and a myopic and dangerous one at that. When has it ever been good that one man makes all the decisions. Never.

Education in China lacks a global perspective, it remains insular, biased, and racial. It stereotypes and denies history, including, or perhaps especially, the iniquities perpetrated by Russian and Chinese Communism. Stereotyping discourages rational thought. It is forbidden history. This is frightening and dangerous. Parents who allow their children to be taught hate will find out that eventually their children will learn to dismiss them as well.

De-legitimize Xi Jinping by expanding access for Chinese Nationals to Western educational networks and combine this with loan relief. Accompany this with an expanded trade program that doesn't just offshore but supports and protects Western manufacturing excellence. This will break free a large segment of Chinese youth from their indecisiveness about a President who said they should "eat bitterness". This will lead them to search for alternatives or demand alterations to Xi Jinping's system of governance.

1.7 million Chinese are incarcerated, the second highest prison population in the world, second only to United States. President Jinping is destined to grow this population segment which will result in a political system that defies reform or relief for all citizens. Xi Jinping has proclaimed that the Soviet System failed because it became ideologically complacent. He emphasizes that the Party must be used as an instrument of social compliance. The Soviet Union though did not dissolve because of a failure to adhere to orthodoxy. It failed because Communism is inherently irrational and requires a surveillance society to prop up the illogic of its political structure. What is needed in China is not a reflexive tightening of controls, but instead an opening up of Chinese civil society to the promise of a productive re-engagement with the World – a world that would readily welcome and a absorb the best of Chinese tradition into their own cultural framework. It would be a worldwide flowering of diversity and would herald in a new era of global human potential.

At the other end the Chinese demographic spectrum the elderly are being subject to gradual reductions in benefits that will soon reach an inflection point, where it is realized that President Jinping's program of exclusion, is designed to disadvantage them as well. A media campaign that highlights Communist Party Politburo hypocrisy in this area should be aggressively pursued. Combine this with a criticism of the current program of prescriptive relief, and you will have created a public relations campaign that demonstrates that independence for the elderly Chinese citizen is sacrificed in the name of a higher and amorphously defined communist party imperative that favors membership.

Late life stage Chinese citizens feel dismissed socially and must be shown that their lifelong sacrifices to China are under-valued, and renumerated at levels that does not recognize the contributions they provided to China's current success. Programs that offer partial relief are often more frustrating than no program at all. They stratify and segment this population. This group remains malleable in that their vulnerabilities can quickly be transformed into an awareness that they have been permanently forgotten by a system of government controlled by one man.

On the other hand the participation issue for younger voters is not apathy, but disinterest. Youth are inherently restive and therefore are impressionable. The challenge will be to provide them concrete examples of how their transition towards independence is fostered and nurtured by a Nation that allows them to expose opportunities that exist outside of government control. Highlight that their participation as citizens in the West requires responsibility but also incorporates an acknowledgment that they can make a difference when they are allowed to explore career alternatives as a principle of self-determination.

The ability to dissent should not be described as a palliative, but rather reframed from a long-term perspective that offers the promise of near-term support from Western Institutions, not only for ideas that criticize, but that also offer solutions and alternatives. President Jinping's administration needs to be described as not offering an opportunity to disagree because the Party rejects these ideas have value to their communities and families. Party criticism of divergence from doctrine is to be equated as a lack of support, respect and concern for the individual. Demonstrate that the Party is composed of spinless hypocrites who lie to gain support.

How then to re-enamor Chinese youth with a renewed enthusiasm for Diversity and Openness. K-Pop is a replicable and irresistible example, but the pull of American multi-cultural inclusiveness also provides opportunity. Media designed to show case classic American acceptance of innovative ideas but that also wonders at the beauty of the Chinese cultural experience and then embraces China as a complementary global relative will prove the lack of insight that hobbles the Xi Jinping regime. The Indian diaspora was allowed to create Olympian levels of wealth in the United States. Why not the untapped brain trusts of China? Who would benefit? Everyone! With one exception, 2 bitter and isolated old men who think that only by their divine right to lead will their countries become pre-eminent. The blunt reality is that the United States was the catalyst that created China's wealth, and that the US can take it away, but both nations would be diminished.

Emphasize the value of the individual to Country and to Democratic processes of inclusion. Highlight how Communist programs are meant to pull the People off balance. Show how new parents, and their parents, will struggle to create a better future for their children in a system meant to allocate benefits based on connections as opposed to opportunity. This would be a powerful message that isolates Communist policy as deeply uncaring and unfair.

What should be of greater concern are far right Communist true believers who exhibit intractable irrationality. Let's just acknowledge a deeply uncomfortable characteristic of many of President Jinping's supporters, that they are warped by xenophobia, or simply lack moral resilience. Both incline them to being receptive to messages of hate and grievance. Xi Jinping offers them an excuse and outlet to relieve themselves of responsibility for their behavior and beliefs. These individuals crave acceptance and because of it will readily pledge themselves to the President without a consideration of affect. This segment of the public is also prone to rationalizing violence as a way of further relieving them from responsibility for current circumstances.

The Communist Party must be isolated and differentiated from other international examples of governance. This requires a repudiation of Xi Jinping's behavior and actions that needs to be conveyed as irredeemable. Extremists need to be portrayed as the foundation of his support while emphasizing that their behavior is aberrant and abhorrent. Communist Party pronouncements that support predatory economic practices, military aggression in the Indo-Pacific, and a disregard for human rights are deplorable, but none more so than the anti-communist and imperialist support that is provided for Putin in Ukraine. Xi Jinping does this so transparently as a prelude towards legitimizing his designs on Taiwan, and in so doing joins the disgrace that is Putin - and Trump. It is weakness parading as strength in all three men.

President Jinping has been described as a camouflaged narcissist, and he is obviously self-absorbed and selfish. How could he not be as the purported author of 120 books that tediously expound on the virtues his character and of Chinese communist ideology. Likely it is from this perspective that he develops his zero-sum perspective on society. He describes an international system that is manipulated to the advantage of a few, a cabal of conspirators. Never mind that this is a political construct that he actively works to achieve. He states that others manipulate the system to their advantage with the inevitable consequence that they take what was needed by others. This then provides an opportunity for those who are inordinately self-absorbed to lose themselves in the big Xi Jinping lie that outside forces are coopting government.

Deng Xiaoping protagonists must parade these ideas as intending to create fear. That they are the pronouncements of a lazy and myopic man. President Jinping's acolytes will proselytize more loudly as a result, but this is not undesirable in that it serves to further emphasize that the man they support is to be questioned as unfit to lead. The same must be done in America, and in Russia.

Minorities have already proven to be a worrying challenge for President Jinping. He acknowledges them through insult, disparagement, re-education, and segregation. It is an appeal wrapped in racism, and strangely offers minorities a fig leaf of recognition while holding them out as not conforming to the promise of Communism because they are economic parasites.

As minority population segments achieve higher standards of living they lose their isolating compact with prejudice and become more frustrated the closer they come to full integration. They feel more intensely social exclusions the nearer they are to achieving inclusion. This is why Uyghurs, Tujia, Yi, Hui, and Manchu are becoming more vocal in their demands for full inclusion, a dangerous and potentially disastrous circumstance for President Jinping. It is in this way that minority segments of China become sensitive to the message of Shehui Guhua. They are forced to reconsider their relationship with a Communism that refuses to meet them where they live culturally and demographically. What industrialized democracies must do is highlight examples of the prosperity, community, and support that would otherwise be provided to them by welcoming Western communities, along with an illustration of the Communist hypocrisy preventing the same.

This needs to be presented not just conceptually, but also with concrete examples of how the US Democratic melting pot brings about improvements in quality of life while respecting cultural tradition. Diversity is America's greatest strength, which is why Donald Trump is America's greatest danger. Interestingly, this danger is being replicated in President Jinping. The two men will eventually meet in a self-reinforcing strategy to cancel each other out. The result will be war.

Hukou cannot be managed without increasing the costs of social control. Managed migration creates discontent. Stratified unemployment, especially among the young, plants the seeds of political civil disobedience. The cost will be the militarization of China as President Jinping uses this vehicle to tamp down dissent and impose social control. Otherwise, what other option does he have? Bureaucratic oversight that is not intrusive but that also coordinates with other support programs would facilitate a reincorporation of this citizen back into the economic framework. The destitute need to be subsidized. It is not enough to propose these changes. They must be actively championed, otherwise the complete lack of concern exhibited by corrupt Party practices will quickly overwhelm any criticism President Jinping suffers as the leader of the Communist Party.

What the West must provide is an acknowledgment that these concerns are valid and need to be resolved. This also implies that minorities cannot be treated monolithically. Any recognition of this fact would do much to undermine President Jinping's legitimacy. The first nation to do this meaningfully gains their support, which will be achieved at the expense of President Jinping as the legitimate leader of a nation forcefully compressed into One People.

Propose, from the White House, the creation of a Chinese cultural heritage Museum. Champion every successful ex-patriot, as well as the hard road to recognition that the diaspora has experienced here in the US. Tank Man must be recognized and honored by the President with the Medal of Freedom. Honor the dead of Tiananmen Square. Return cultural artifacts that were removed from China without permission. Can you imagine the impact? China would dissolve into a paroxysm of gratitude (and manufactured outrage). The intuition the US President would exhibit in honoring Chinese contributions to the American cultural experience, along with an acknowledgement of the historical shame of Sino Racism, would make this action ring throughout history. It would restore faith domestically and internationally in the idea of America, and more importantly in the promise of China. It would demonstrate that we all can be a shining beacon of hope and promise, and that the entire world would benefit from a welcoming incorporation of China into the World community. All the more reason to acknowledge that President Jinping and Trump are the wrong leaders at the wrong time, and that we all need to work for a peaceful removal of both men.

GOOD BIRD, BAD TREE 良禽择木而栖，贤臣择主而事

5

Wise leaders hire capable partners. Why then is it that both President Jinping and President Trump appear to select lieutenants who overtly sycophantic? This is because the Criminal has a peculiar place in the appeal provided by an Autocratic Populist – especially one who can claim kinship with them. Chauvinism offers the corrupt redemption, and when blame can be placed on social structures and circumstance, an ardent adherent of both President's is the result.

Americans vote based on haircut styles and slogans. In China support is provided based on coercion and cooption. In America a vote can be more easily relinquished based on a joke or insult than it would in terms of the quality of a candidate's character, experience, or devotion to duty. In China support is bought by bestowing privilege via a cult of personality embraced by the power of propaganda. This sorry state is further corrupted when money remains the primary motivator in politics. Party members who can attribute their success more to quid pro quo than to the quality of their obligations attracts the worst of China to public service. Party programs are populated with unknown and unknowable beneficiaries. Communist initiatives are designed to imply one thing but implement another. It is impossible in many instances to discern their real intent.

Many in China lack either the will or the interest to research issues and motivations that exist beyond their community in any case. Most simply acquiesce and hope for the best. At its worst their support is relinquished without any consideration for its effect. Irrelevance in citizenship has created an ennui of disinterest, where the impression is that constituent opinions are ignored in favor of those who can purchase influence. Simply said why bother to disagree or campaign for change.

In putting down the Tiananmen protest, the Communist Party embedded a way for the average citizen to harbor resentment and allow distrust to fester. Why Deng Xiaoping put down a protest with a slaughter was a confounding and incomprehensible policy blunder, a staggering tragedy that will require national reconciliation, which President Jinping will obviously never initiate. This continues to provide dissatisfied Chinese with an excuse to disengage. They are imbued with the idea that in the future they could be potential martyrs to change.

This is unfortunately also an effective means for generating unity of purpose in individuals who have already relinquished their freedom of thought by rationalizing the event in order to consolidate support around a cause that is described as greater than the protested concerns. What this provides President Jinping is the opportunity to further consolidate his control over the Communist party, a party which divides, conquers, and consolidates power in Xi.

As President Jinping continues to radicalize his comments he takes these calls to action to an extreme. He markets himself as a great Leader who deserves praise and loyalty, and if needed to be followed as a necessary change agent of violence. His threats to do this are no longer vague. He incarcerates and implies the threat of violence as a response to perceived threats. In fact it is necessary that he do this for the simple reason that organizations formed around a peaceful purpose are comprised of individuals who contribute based on individualized interpretations of intent. On the other hand a movement that initiates a call to action with the possibility of the application of force is more compact and also more cohesive. It is the structure required by a group that subsumes individuality to the movement.

This is the direction in which President Jinping is taking the Party. To create an organization based on directed action that will attempt to re-initiate a Maoist insurrectionist movement – but this time one inevitably organized by violence externally oriented to initiate change. And by change meaning not just the realization of a President Jinping Imperial Presidency, but the full imposition of a President Jinping political machine at all levels of the political process that can then by exported internationally. This is the true danger presented by Xi Jinping. Not that he maintains his tenure as General Secretary, but that he continues to consolidate control over the political machine that is China. His conversion of the Presidency into a new Maoist populist autocracy puts the entire world at risk. Unfortunately, the only response the Democracies of the World will have in the short term is to further isolate China economically, which puts China on a collision course with America as it attempts to maintain access to any resources and markets that remain to it.

Can there be any doubt that once Xi Jinping consolidates control over every level of social, economic and political aspects of the Chinese cultural experience that he will pervert them to an imposition of a Chinese hegemony on the rest of the world? His accusations of a corrupted western world view become his means for tearing down the entire international system in support of his desire to appoint China as the pre-eminent nation within the global firmament.

The Master Plan or Strategic Roadmap that President Jinping is constructing for China will incorporate short term compromises with the US, but Trump being the puerile political incompetent narcissist that he is will misinterpret this as an example of his ability to negotiate success on the international stage. What happens next is that President Jinping will use this to relax the diplomatic footing of the US, and then initiate low grade aggressive actions against Taiwan. At first these efforts will be ignored, but by then this pattern of violence will inure the United States, i.e. Trump, to his intent, at which point the US will express outrage, but from a distance At that point the de-facto reabsorption of Taiwan into the Chinese political framework will have begun. Trump in all of his glorious glowing orange incompetence will have been the catalyst that allowed this to happen.

There is no way an all-out attack on Taiwan will succeed if replied to in kind, and President Jinping knows this. Rather the initiation of an implication of violence will underscore an outrageous impertinence that will serve to legitimize the rationale of his argument that Taiwan must be re-united with the mainland at almost any cost. This is a tactic used by every Populist, and numerous 20th century examples can be used to underscore this fact. As for our 21st century example now being undertaken in Ukraine, can there be any doubt that Putin will fail? Success was not his only intent. Rather as is the case with Trump and the January 6th attack on American Capital, the goal is to focus outrage and discontent that is also used as an excuse to aggressively and violently initiate internal actions to quash discontent and consolidate political power. The danger for any of these actions is that they gestate counter vailing internal inclinations to rebel, the restlessness being too hard to contain. The Wagner group is an example of this, and there is just such a group waiting in the wings in China as well.

What has changed in the modern era, is that Tenured Democratic Presidents, Imperial Party Chairman, and Communist Autocrats can now all diminish freedoms by automating a 'Fengqiao' model of community supervision via artificially generated intelligent systems that will dramatically expand capabilities in targeted surveillance. A program revived from the time of Mao, that now includes menstruation tracking programs. Xi will expand the efficacy of monitoring capabilities from the current benchmark of 15 million people to the entire population of 1.4 billion Chinese via large language models that will surface phrases that imply dissent. No longer will it be necessary to sift out potential opposition to party policy. Instead, AI determined probability models will calculate dissent probabilities, which will then be used by Chinese Thought Police to cut down organized movements before they coalesce. China will be the first to successfully accomplish this.

In the first 6 months of 2024 the Chinese judicial system prosecuted 31,000 people for the crime of 'spreading rumors'. The process has already begun. Democracies of the World take note. You are next.

Government control will be unleashed at the level of the individual and their community. Compliance will be accomplished via controlled access to social programs, educational systems, and employment opportunities. Trump will also do this by abolishing employment security for US bureaucracies and replacing 'treacherous' professionals with faithful Trump supporters who will be willing to subvert American principles of privacy in the name of National Security. He will do this to degrade the independence of these organizations and place himself a step closer to a tenured American President.

Putin has already accomplished this via the creation of a clearly corrupt and captured Russian Oligarchy. President Jinping is in the process of doing the same via his program of controlled access to Party Privilege. All three men will use economic levers of power to exert social control to consolidate political power. They appear to be competitors, and for a while they will be, but in the end will form a triarchy of Oceania, Eurasia, and East Asia, that provides an appearance of enmity, but which in actuality is designed to channel antagonism as a vehicle of social control.

What we will experience is the carving up the planet into resource zones of control that equate prosperity with a militarization of resource aggrandizement. What will follow will be an attempt to control space, and a degradation of this planet's ability to sustain quality of life. By then the die will be cast. War, social fragmentation, and the loss of mankind's future potential will be expressed in a regression back into a state of survival of the fittest that will herald the beginning of the end of the Promise of Man.

All three men possess an intractable psychopathic capacity for self-rationalization. Putin, while powerful internally, lacks an ability to move his capacity for influence internationally. His current effort in Ukraine will fail. Trump, while clearly stunted emotionally and suspect mentally, will hopefully be countered by a still robust American bi-cameral system. President Jinping on the other hand does not possess these limitations or restrictions. He is a Master of his Craft, and destined to do great things, terrible but great. Thus the inflection point for China becomes the inflection point for the world. This is the deep danger posed by President Jinping if he is permitted to continue unrestrained for life in office.

Tenured Presidencies are indeed dangerous, and they inevitably lead to violence. And while violence of action sometimes does not succeed it provides a benefit to the Populist in that it grows in scope and aggressiveness and eventually spreads, ultimately affecting the entire nation and its military. This circumstance remains a deep danger for an unrestrained President that could lead, however preposterous the idea may seem now, to the overt imposition of a new Chinese imperialism based on resource monopolization that is backed by an irresistible Chinese militarism. Confronted by this deep danger to American Hegemony, Trump and his successors will strive to do the same.

The spontaneity and violence of an attack on Taiwan would de-legitimize President Jinping to the rest of the world but solidify him as a messianic Chinese Leader to his People. It will reinforce the idea among them that America must be countered and will provide the rationale for continuing deliberate action. A cause ordained by an idea of Chinese Manifest destiny. Never mind that President Jinping holds the Chinese people in contempt. It only matters that they feel they belong to a great cause, one ordained by China's new autocratic populist.

From this President Jinping will make further attempts to de-legitimize current international political relationships. In fact he needs to do so in order to maintain the momentum of his support. Without this his movement would fracture and then dissipate within isolated pockets of crazy conspiracists who would be watched closely but otherwise will be regarded with disdain by the international community. These fragmented groups would then once again go underground until a new Populist reorganizes them and masticates the sense that they are failures into a hate for an America, their voices unleashed to become shills for ignorance.

In this way hate will become an important part of President Jinping's diatribe and is why his supporters will readily mimic his style. Hate is a unifier for President Jinping. His acolytes adopt this approach because it is easy. Their laziness speaks to the personal corruption of their character, much like the Communist Pretender they support. These dialectical disciples of destruction must be continuously refreshed by outrage and derision, keeping them in a constant state of readiness for action.

The President Jinping acolyte gives up a right to be discrete. To confront them provides them with an excuse for action, an excuse for aggression. It renders them even more impervious to a consideration of alternatives. It is a reinforcement of a process of self-renunciation that Xi Jinping continually reinforces. His supposed spontaneous acts of shock and awe are in actuality designed to perpetuate his supporters' inclination to reject individualized action. It surfaces within them a readiness for 'trial by combat'. President Jinping invents a feeling within his supporters that they are integral to a restoration of the Chinese ideal, hence party members who adhere to regimented conversations that do not stray from orthodoxy, or who pretend to be dogmatic Marxists.

Even more ominous are the community grid management monitoring programs set up by CCP where whole neighborhoods are carved up into 15 to 20 households per monitoring segment, and where residents are asked to report on their neighbors. These 'grid workers' engage in a childlike display that has no meaning or substance other than to confirm that they are cowards who through this expression of loyalty reveal that they can be manipulated. Rest assured that Donald Trump will look with interest on this method of social control. Already news articles in the US are warning of his ability to subvert privacy rules by gaining access to cell phone conversations. This 'grid system' of neighbor monitoring neighbor is ready made to be automated via AI like Co-Pilot Agents that create virtual reporting neighborhoods where relationships are prepositioned to generate surveillance alerts. This future proliferates Co-Pilot Monitoring Agents that automate a '3 Degrees of Separation' surveillance society to assure political compliance by surfacing dissention, starting at the level of the individual, instantly overlaid with their virtually established electronic neighborhood.

Crime Prevention is then merged with Social Control. Freedom of thought becomes an imposition that is monitored and surveilled using an electronic form Hukou. This is the future vision of Xi Jinping - a version of Chinese Manifest Destiny that will be offered to the rest of the world. This is a clear and present danger that will diminish the dynamism of the human experience for the entire planet. No nation will suffer more from this than China itself – the new birthplace of manufactured cultural homogeneity and mediocrity. President Jinping will have replaced the magnificence of his nation's cultural diversity with a pride in the conforming capabilities of technological prowess. Its epicenter will be the blanching of China's magnificent multi-cultural historical heritage.

The pathetic nature of neighbor reporting on neighbors could be ignored if it were not so dangerous. In the US the web site Nextdoor also demonstrates this inclination towards a de-evolution of neighborhood civility, where complaints, rumors, character destruction, and nasty reports on one's neighbors has subsumed the website's original intent of support, cooperation and a sharing of community resources. All of this underscores a routinization of the worst of human nature in social media both in the US and China, a process unleashed by America but which will be brought to fruition in China.

President Jinping and President Trump have already used these communication vehicles to inculcate an obedience so extreme that if it degenerates into violence they will both excuse it as resulting from crimes manufactured by opponents, but which they themselves will have set in motion. In this way President Jinping is truly a pressing peril not only for China, but for rest of the world, as other populist leaders mimic his social technologies, beginning with Trump. In this way Xi Jinping will have achieved his goal of a preeminent China, to the determinant of the rest of the world.

What President Jinping is blazing is a path for other Autocrats to follow. It is an initiation into the cult of President Jinping at the level of world leadership. These men will become part of a corrupted leadership club of Autocrats that imparts injurious consequence globally as they all attempt to impart meaning to their narcissism and lust for power.

What Populist leaders do is work to foment (or leverage) domestic instability to generate support. Such men must be countered by shedding light on their motivations by strengthening bicameral or parliamentary structures that isolate their inclination towards fascism and demagoguery, starting with Judicial frameworks that put a break on chaos generating autocratic political frameworks. Principles of privacy must be respected. Media must be de-consolidated.

Multi-media needs to be legally constrained by prohibiting automated linking recommendations. As an example in the US, American Nazis could still link to other White Nationalists, but they would have to do so manually.

Otherwise automatically generated multi-media recommendations will become the foundation of virtual 'neighborhood grid' electronic surveillance systems of social control. They will also continue to self-reinforce the worst inclinations of human nature. Prevented in the US, this then will isolate China as it progresses further into multi-media homogeneity. Nothing could be more effective at putting a brake on the diffusion of Chinese AI based cultural manipulation, beginning with Tik-Tok, as China finds itself increasingly at odds in a world that rejects fascism and welcomes openness and diversity. China would once again find itself isolated, an untenable circumstance for the newly enlightened Chinese global citizen.

President Jinping's and President Trump's doctrines have become a stronghold for the politically derelict, a ghetto for the mindless and ignorant. It is impervious to criticism, and the rational holds no relevance for its adherents. The strength a Xi Jinping's acolyte feels comes not from within himself but from a feeling that he is part of something more powerful than himself. The innate strength that any stoic individual possesses is invalidated. Commitment is derived from a despondency that orients itself into a desire to break the will of perceived opponents who would frustrate their goals for economic security. It is an attempt to validate a rejection of self-determination. President Jinping becomes a substitute for God, his party for the Church. What follows is a rejection of all that exists external to this commitment. China becomes supreme. Isolationist tendencies are unavoidable corollaries of this affect. It has no consideration for what is good for China but rather for what consolidates power in President Jinping.

Isolated the average Chinese citizen feels ineffectual, but as part of the Communist Party they are mobilized and actualized to support orthodoxy as unassailable. What President Jinping does is offer the Party Member participatory alternatives that claim to recognize their worth. Otherwise they feel further isolated and reviled. A powerful motivator to comply. The only immediate way to counter this will be to render their Communist figurehead ridiculous, a parody of Mao, even unfortunately to the point of conspiracy. President Jinping is to be made into a clown, a red clown, with a ridiculous and stone faced countenance that is a parody of strength. Portray him in all of his pathetic vanity as an ordained leader and he will be revealed as noxious and worthy of derision and ridicule. It is an unsavory tactic, but it would work.

Counter President Jinping with a parade of Patriots who praise the Deng Xiaoping tradition of honoring Chinese ingenuity and inclusion. Praise a diaspora that can rejuvenate China culturally. Demonstrate that China's great national experiment succeeded because the nation, through Deng Xiaoping (as did the Soviet Union through Khrushchev), rejected demagogues and can do so again. In fact while President Jinping attempts to manifest a mandate connected to the past, instead aggressively connect him to historical past tragedies that are now gratefully rejected, such as the national tragedy of the Great Leap Forward, while also acknowledging that Deng Xiaoping's greatest mistake was the Tiananmen Square

Massacre, an event that President Jinping has never denounced.

Demonstrate that Xi Jinping practices the disgrace of cronyism and welcomes the corruption of money. Reveal that he implies validity in eugenics, and that he does not denounce the shame of Maoist corruption or the disgrace that is Tiananmen. Shame him for his dog whistle that foreign powers will "get their heads bashed if they attempt to bully or influence the country". This is the immodesty that is Xi Jinping. A complementary China internationally will deliver have far more wide-ranging benefits for nation (and the world) than that provided by militaristic posturing. Proclaim it loudly.

President Jinping imitates Mao, which is a disgrace. Trump admires Andrew Jackson, a proponent of American Imperialism, a supporter of slavery, and a promoter of Indian Genocide – also a disgrace.

The illogic of their historical perspective means their pronouncements contain no basis in fact other than that they generate an impression in their supporters that they are no longer dismissed and forgotten by a system described as perpetuating an unfairness in a distribution of benefits. To some extent this has a basis in fact from an entrenchment of profit and power perspective, and a disenfranchisement of the destitute, all while lower economic segments of China and America are asked to self-actualize in the face of dislocation. In fact Communist Party characterizations of support for rural China in terms of programs that trade prosperity for security can and should be portrayed as camouflage for monied interests which deign to maintain power at the expense of those constituencies they are meant to serve.

President Jinping's fantasy is a histrionic melodramatic gesture that manufactures slights and turns them in to crimes. Exaggerated theatrics is no stranger to populist movements. The more frightfully extreme they become, the more the message becomes the movement.

However irrelevant slogans like the 'Two Establishes' and the 'Two Upholds' are, the more appealing the message becomes. The more ostentatious the message the more effective it becomes at gaining an audience. This is why President Jinping rails at non-compliance with communist orthodoxy, and why the garbage of his rhetoric must be used to construct counter points after each and every Presidential pronouncement. In the West his statements are dismissed as lacking relevance, but that is not the intent. President Jinping's statements are not designed to inform but to induce compliance. Bleach his message with ex-patriots who represent an expansive offshore Chinese consciousness that forms a distinct and opposing perspective.

President Jinping is bland and uninteresting because he needs to be. He is a deconstructed Populist. He does not stand out because has nothing else to stand on. Creating a spectacle would foster an atmosphere of gallantry. Instead he implies that he is sacrificing himself for the body politic when in fact he is defacing the Chinese political system with the graffiti of his autocratic populist

Maoist garbage. It is transparent but effective. If on the other hand he were to convey himself as a man of veracity willing to work within the system, he would immediately lose his hold on the CCP because he would no longer have anything to offer his supporters. The opportunity he provides is to lose themselves in a program of excuses designed to absolve them of self-determination.

This is felt most keenly by the new Zhongguoren who have experienced some marginal sense of success but perceive that they are being mistreated by a detached privileged conspiracy of elites. They would not be completely unjustified in this perception, and it is in this way that Communist Party privilege works to President Jinping's disadvantage. To the Jinping acolyte and indeed for many aspiring members of the Communist Party, the Party becomes the problem, not the solution.

Xi Jinping playacts at leadership, but he has yet to flesh out his performances with new emblems. It will not be until revives a Chinese led Comintern trademarked with a new symbol of International Communism that he will have fully morphed over from populism to autocratic communist based fascism.

China remains vulnerable to symbols of power and hate. Freedom of Speech remains a privilege not a right, and as an endemic aspect of human nature, China is not immune to racism as exhibited by characterizations such as Leftard, Xiao Riben, Yang Guizi, Bangzi, and Tai Bazi. The United States also suffers from this embarrassment of ignorance as was seen during the anti-Jewish Tiki Torch rally in Charlottesville, shamefully dismissed as unimportant by an American President who is also a Felon convicted of sexual assault. Deceit is programmatic in every Populist and President Jinping is not an exception. As ritual becomes an increasingly important part of President Jinping's program of deception, one will see structured demonstrations of obeisance that devolve into demonstrations of hate.

President Jinping reinforces this by manufacturing a myth of mighty acts that were performed by Chinese Communists in response to corrupt western hegemonies. He allows this to be described by using imagery of self-sacrifice. These falsifications are convincing because they create belief without fact. Rationalization with false syllogism. This is part of the exhibitionist disgrace that is President Jinping, which is now imitated by his supporters.

Pretending is a necessary part of his program. It is unassailable because it is contrary to logic. What must be provided to China is an excuse to strip away the veil from Xi Jinping's persona as a warrior for Chinese Communism. He must be revealed to be the weak and corrupt individual that he is. A trait he shares with Trump.

Despicable figures who offer him praise, criminals, the vacuous, and those who otherwise inspire disgust must also be disparaged. This includes the fawning support he receives from sanctified officials. Provide an offramp for his less intransigent supporters. This will loosen his grip on a public that otherwise breathlessly waits for his next insult and lie.

Remove the disguise that hides President Jinping's weaknesses. Parade those who have been hurt by his actions in front of the Chinese public. His reactions will become more strident and irrational, and this will weaken him. Exacerbate his narcissism. Keep it stoked. Insult him. He lives in a bubble of lies and vacuous accolades. Implode the facade of his persona by using his narcissism against him. It is his greatest weakness. Deny his egotism and limited perspective legitimacy. Make it embarrassing. It will create in him a lunacy which will dismay the nation.

SLOW COOKED FROGS 井底之蛙

6

President Jinping by necessity must commend the present structure of Government. He twists it from something constructive into a millennial techno-utopian dialectic hallucination, thereby offering him a platform for the excuses that he uses to dismiss any criticism of his tenured Presidency. His close-minded perspective on China's many iniquities are directly attributable to his leadership. This is why a disciplined and routinized release of his personal political, social, and economic failures needs be politicized by Chinese ex-patriots. They must also represent the demographic aspirations of President Jinping's base. Do this in terms of the impact his failures have had on the life of others. Bankruptcies, firings, ethnic cleansings, bride prices, abortions of female fetuses. All need to be conveyed as failures of policy due to his character.

His hypocrisy must be conveyed not only in terms of the causes he champions, but in also terms of the fragmented nature of his personality. His support of a murderous North Korian regime. His alliance with a criminal Russian Oligarchy. It is not enough to say he lies. The injuries he causes others are real and need to be advertised. Only then will he be shown to possess an uncaring character that is abhorrent. President Jinping's personality is unclean. His detestation of his opponents must be refocused into a refutation of his character.

President Jinping deliberately portrays the American experience as being one of misery because he must. It is premeditated because otherwise his program would be uninteresting. He is in some ways an unlikely entertainer, and while his message is often one subtly infused with resentment, hate, and anger, this is precisely why his supporters identify with him as a sanctified leader. He is their President, a representative personification of their personal frustration.

The derision he breeds for foreigners serves to further emphasize the isolation his supporters feel, and the sense of belonging they derive from the same. Ending the helplessness that the Jinping supporter feels needs to become an operative part of a foreign relations campaign. Done effectively with an emphasis that President Jinping takes without giving back will start the process. Examples of Xi Jinping's doctrine of heads I win, tails you lose, can be found everywhere in his cultural appeals. Conveyed in terms of injuries experienced, including importantly his pseudo communist doctrine of dialectic capitalism, will go a long way towards loosening his grip on what is otherwise a beguiled audience.

Highlight the embarrassing qualities of his persona, but also ridicule his most extreme supporters. They do not constitute the majority of his base and must be represented as laughable examples of his doctrine. Contempt for the extreme behavior of his base will begin to rub off as contempt for the man, an individual utterly devoid of original thoughts, actions, and deeds.

President Jinping's proclamations for the future are neither workable nor feasible and only offer the option of an aggrandizement of power in one man. The West needs to provide more granular examples of the power disparities that exist between President Jinping as a member of the privileged elite and those who are financially disadvantaged. Demonstrate how he misuses bankruptcy laws and injures those he constrains economically. Show how the benefit accrued to his favored elite alone. Provide examples of his willingness to sacrifice others in favor of his own personal advantage.

Create an offramp to redirect support for a China which opens its arms to the World.

Demagogues on the other hand always look to refocus blame and stipulate that the path to a celebrated future must be accompanied by a destruction of the conspiratorial criminality of the present. The implication is that the corrupt will not relinquish power without violence. Hate can then be channeled by the Demagogue into aggression, a necessary corollary to gaining control of the disaffected. It becomes more than an addicting mixture of a shared affinity of purpose and self-sacrifice. It is a balm for the despondency of its adherents. This sharing of hate ironically is converted into hope that becomes a salve that redeems the worthless. Purpose joins with promise to relieve the insecurity of those who perceive themselves as lacking political value.

A fomenter of revolution develops a myth of the past connected to an ideal of a millennial future. In this way their acolytes can turn their back on the present. It is a fabrication of past glory that is used as a rejection of the here and now. When these ideas of the past are connected to a redemption of the future, continuity of concept is established that requires a destruction of the present. In this way the present is deprived of its authenticity, rendering it impervious to argument and entreaties for compromise. The members of these movements see themselves as sanctified warriors imbued with chants and flags that convey the belief that they are the elect who have been chosen to champion a great cause. When this morphs into self-sacrifice and is couched in the lexicon of a willingness to be imprisoned or even die for the cause, the movement is poised to scale up into organized violence as a necessary prerequisite for goal achievement.

The constituents of a mass movement set their eyes on areas of vulnerability in the present. Imbalance and iniquity are used as a rationale to delegitimize and imply that the entire structure is rotten and needs to be torn down. Implications of a corrupted judicial or economic system are used to convey the idea that the entire system is being jury rigged to foster dissent. It then becomes an obligation of the individual to crusade for radical reform in support of the Peoples Republic. This delegitimization of local government becomes a gateway for the formation of a mass movement motivated by a Populist. Rational proponents of change are described as lacking insight and a commitment to the spirit of Marxist–Leninism, which further compels the disenchanted to seek out a promise of guaranteed glory.

Traditionally a Communist Proselytizer implies that the present can be bettered by enforcing Communist dogma, or past principles of orthodoxy. This is another reason why President Jinping has been able to dominate the Party. He rejects the present and delegitimizes it claiming that the current state of affairs is being irredeemably damaged by an external liberal dynamic. It is a state of affairs where the conservative champions for a renovation of the present.

President Jinping's goal is to also sever loyalty to the Deng Xiaoping image of a tolerant China and remake it into an authoritarian facsimile dedicated to a strong leader centered on himself. This is why the incredulity expressed about where Communist principles of sacrifice can be found are irrelevant to Xi Jinping. Everything is flipped on its head. Left is Right and Right is Left. Communism is Capitalism. Neither approach is portrayed as having legitimacy when allowed to interact. Only the Party of President Jinping is described as having the solution and indeed the obligation to lead the nation into the future. In this way Xi Jinping subsumes the principles of Marx and Engles into an obligation to support him as the next leader of destiny. As the Party continues to compromise more traditional Communist principles President Jinping will further consolidate power and all of China will find that have surrendered to him as well.

Liberal and Conservative can be further extrapolated using President Jinping's perspective on human nature. President Jinping is willful and self-centered and because he sees this in himself, he also assumes this is an intractable aspect of every personality. Others cannot be trusted or depended on because he himself holds no loyalties other than to himself. This is the reason why Xi Jinping pursues the path of distrust, and why Deng Xiaoping emphasized the practicable. Deng Xiaoping believed the human spirit was weak, but that it could be rehabilitated with forceful discipline. For President Jinping, trust is the harbinger of destruction.

There is a solution, albeit a dangerous one, as Trump will soon so rudely realize. As each leader steps in the cesspool of the other's rhetoric they will find that at first each will playact at reconciliation, but eventually Trump through his surrogates will stoke President Jinping's intransigence. The more stridently obstinate President Jinping becomes the more irrational will be Trump's pronouncements, and eventually he and President Jinping will be enraged to the point of senseless foolishness, thereby subjecting them both to ridicule. When this happens President Jinping will find Trump to be at his most vulnerable, and Jinping will stoke this intransigence until Trump implodes under the weight of his own indignation.

Stupid is as stupid does and Trump will attempt to use President Jinping's assertions against him. He will do this against a backdrop of MAGA obscenity, and attempt less than flattering pronouncements that portray the CCP as the new Axis of Evil. Trump will combine this with a tincture of conspiracy and Communist all-consuming global greed. President Jinping's supporters will cry foul, but the perpetrator of this outrage will be ignored by President Jinping. Trump's vanity will be his undoing. All the while President Jinping will slowly re-position China to take on the World.

President Jinping needs to be portrayed as an aberration, a gross parody of the Communist ideal. To the degree he parrots an idea of sacrifice for orthodoxy, deface the image he has of himself as an enlightened Communist champion of change. Ruthlessly even recklessly portray him as a disease on the Chinese body politic. President Jinping will incline to violence as he approaches the limits of what he can absorb regarding the defacement of the radiance he believes surrounds him. If he resorts to violence internally either directly or through suggestion he will lose the support of the People. Attach every extreme action to him. Emphasize his disregard for past Chinese communist generated tragedies. This will send him into a spiral of contradiction. His uncompromising nature will be his undoing.

President Jinping's constituency currently is more compliantly reactionary than radical. They take delight in the envy they create in others. Their grievances become predictable and are designed to unnerve those whom they feel they would otherwise need to compete against. President Jinping's 'The Governance of China' gives form to this function which is another reason why he so singularly focuses on compliance. It is not a mark of support but rather an indication of the degree to which his dependents derive satisfaction from the feeling that they are effectively chastising the unelected and placing themselves on a superior footing with them. If the attention span of this audience begins to wane this will indicate that his supporters no longer derive a sense of satisfaction from the idea that past national grievances must be redressed. His program of vengeance will then become pedantic and expose his principles as vacuous and worthless – the machinations of a Populist desperate to escape his own insecurities.

This is why President Jinping must continue to proselytize what is impractical. It justifies the prolific impudence of his rhetoric, without which the chaos he creates internationally renders itself subject to verifiable renunciation. The preposterous for him is an end in and of itself when it comes to the tactics he uses to support his meaningless strategy. In the end China will be denied the restorative power of reconnecting with world and the rejuvenating benefits of diversity. The Nation as a whole will be diminished.

FRIENDS FROM FAR AWAY PLACES 有朋自远方来，不亦乐乎

7

President Jinping considers the Chinese experience an end unto itself. He does this because it is something that he that he can use to embellish his own Pride. He believes China can self-actualize, and is ready to sacrifice others to this cause, a cause geared to gain power, to accumulate wealth, garner accolades and assuage a deep-seated insecurity about China's position in the world. This is demonstrated in his willingness to consider acts of violence in order to achieve his policy goals. President Jinping preys on the hopes and dreams of his supporters who also hope they might achieve this Chinese conceptualization of greatness. What allows President Jinping to mislead his public is his aberrant realization that his arrogance is incapable of compromise. A more operationally gifted expert in economic management would focus their attention on systems and processes and methods of management geared towards maintaining and growing earnings, or balancing resource inputs.

The failed manager on the other hand often feels they are eminently qualified to manifest success in public service. A need to re-confirm their value as a leader becomes the driving force behind this strange state of affairs where failed Managers or Party Members turn Politician. One does not have to look far in the ranks of the Politburo to find failures who use politics as a platform to repair their sense of damaged self-worth. Their ineptitude becomes their motivation for success in the public arena. Their desperation to do so leads them to compromise their ethics in leadership. They become equivocators, rationalizing this as being necessary to accomplish greater goals in support of their service to the Nation. Their only real goal is to turn power and influence into income.

This is why many politicians strut and exhibit excessive pride in their own accomplishments all while pronouncing themselves as servants to the Chinese Communist cause. That they succeed makes them feel they are eminently qualified to lead. From this perspective it should be of no surprise that President Jinping has installed himself as tenured, and no surprise that Party members are ready to compromise their principles and character in support of a man who so clearly is not concerned with their opinions and motivations other than how they might serve his interest.

Communist Party members are motivated by self-interest. Their compulsions reside within an intent to deny their sense that they are part of a wretched present that invalidates them as self-determining individuals. This is all the more potent because they lack a concrete definition of self. What must insinuated is a message that the maintenance of the great Chinese Communist Experiment is in itself a lost cause. One with implications for the entire world and all of humankind.

President Jinping must be portrayed as the Great Deceiver. Equate him in the mind of his followers as an unholy pretender. The worst kind of fraud because it preys on their trust and spirituality. President Jinping uses his position to enforce support. Use this against him to create fear and mistrust in the eyes of his followers.

The inane diatribes of Xi Jinping's doctrine often seem so overtly manipulative and self-serving that it is incomprehensible how anyone could believe or be attracted to the meaningless platitudes that pour from his mouth. But in fact these diatribes are necessary to the

Jinping doctrine of belief. Rather than creating in his supporters a kernel of doubt regarding his veracity, it renders his argument impervious to truth. His pronouncements are extreme and therefore absolute. This creates an obstinacy that protects Jinping from the influence of contrary argument. He then routinely rejects out of hand any considerations that could conflict with his own interpretations of circumstance.

To disavow these pronouncements would be to call in to question the veracity of the man himself and for President Jinping this must not be allowed in a belief system that would otherwise immediately collapse under the weight of its own contradictions.

It is disconcerting to realize the degree to which Xi Jinping will go to reject counter argument. That he acts in this way seems inscrutable and irrational, but this is an acute reality of President Jinping's hold on power. In denying common sense, he repudiates his own personal sense that his message lacks value.

Communist Party members crave incongruity and hang their hats on frivolous gibberish. Their goal is not to comprehend but rather to suspend disbelief. This is also why President Jinping does not explain his goals or provide policy details. To create understanding would be to degrade the power of his message. Making sense of policy renders it programmatic and banal, which is why any attempt to clarify or reveal the empty nature of his promises fails as an appeal to his base. His program of smoke and mirrors cannot be attacked directly because it lacks coherence and is therefore impervious to analysis.

What must be done is to attack the man himself. Show him to be the pretender he is. Call in to question his conception of himself as a Chinese Savior. Strip away his persona and reveal him to be the wrinkled and impotent man that he undoubtedly is. Loosen his grip on the Party. His supporters associate themselves with him to bolster the image they have of themselves. If President Jinping is revealed to be loathsome, the duplicity of his character will induce his supporters to feel a revulsion for him. This will engender a rejection of his persona as an example to be imitated.

The legitimacy and conviction of President Jinping's message is not what must be called to account, but rather certitude in President Jinping as an example of the best China has to offer. He instead must be called to account as the worst example of an entitled Chinese myopic focus on greed and devotion to an accumulation of wealth. He is to be made loathsome. Only in this way can he be turned into an object of ridicule. If this begins to take hold in discussions of President Jinping as a Paramount Leader, he will lose the legitimacy of his position.

President Jinping's acolytes are, as is President Jinping himself, vacuous, because they are intellectually lazy. This is why President Jinping has no interest or inclination to participate in rational arguments or debates. He needs to remain incomprehensible in order to maintain the intractability of his message. To do otherwise would require an academic exercise for which he has neither the time nor the inclination to initiate. The return on this investment would not be worth the time he puts into the effort anyway, and would only serve to confuse his supporters.

This narrow approach to message marketing is also one of his greatest vulnerabilities. Force him to respond to questions about his cultural goals for China, the purpose of Communist academics, his confrontational approach to economics, his suppression of ethical sub-groups. His self-portrayal as a man of the people is his Achillies heal. He will turn livid and incomprehensible in his attempt to hit back. The West must ignore President Jinping as he does this, and instead continue to exhibit a capacity for experience and reason, as a league of nations ready to welcome China into a complementary global community. In this way Xi Jinping can be established as not only unfit, but also narrow minded and narcissistically focused on what he feels is best for China.

Illogic in Communist party academics lacks insight, but more importantly is a lie. Create doubt by stripping away this illusion of relevance. Communism is based on dialectic myth, and in this way party members are highly susceptible to a lampoon of Marxist-Leninism. Start with caricatures of these men as being singular examples of what it means to not be Chinese. Create a representation of these myth makers as a parody of President Jinping, which will dismay the rank and file communist party member and lead them to re-consider their commitment to a cause that no longer offers them an unassailable cost and benefit analysis. Support a con artist and you look like a fool. More importantly you yourself become an object of ridicule. An untenable position for any Xi Jinping supporter.

President Jinping's devotees are deeply insecure. It will take little effort to generate a distaste for the President. Call it what it is, character assassination. This needs to be done not in terms of the lies he creates, but instead as an appeal to party members who will perceive that they have been treated unfairly and overlooked purposefully by Jinping. If they recognize that Xi Jinping sees them as tools to be used and later thrown away, they will turn away from him. Indeed there are many examples of how he has already done so. Highlight this. President Jinping is a stunt. His lieutenants are jokes. Connect President Jinping's disciples to the man as laughably lamentable. Then appeal to them as citizens of a great nation who have been deceived and overlooked but are forgotten no more.

Part of the danger President Jinping poses to China is in the innate characteristic of the movement he created. Sudden change requires a mass movement which responds as a cohesive whole. The unquestioning obedience President Jinping demands also requires a mutability of purpose in his followers, one that can be changed by the President at will. This enables many opportunities for him to turn his movement to violence if it serves his purpose. Indeed he will be unable to prevent it if his support begins to wane and fracture. The vehemence of his rhetoric will increase as he begins to lose his grip on the commitment of his supporters.

The closer China finds itself to a confrontation with the United States the more isolated China will become. The world will unite against President Jinping. Putin will provide tentative support, but he is impotent and therefore meaningless. The smart move, if President Jinping was open minded, would be to revive and expand upon a policy of engagement with the West that was begun by Deng Xiaoping and reinforced by Jiang Zemin. Allow China to flourish in the international arena, and China will embrace the world with the power of her endless energy and capacity to reinvent herself. The alternative is that President Jinping will find himself at risk of losing everything China has accomplished since Deng Xiaoping. Because of it he will be unable to restrain himself from resorting to violence. This is the great fallacy of the efficacy of autocracy, and one of the reasons President Jinping is singularly unfit for Office.

The US will then need to aggrandize allies and coordinate with regional governments to prevent President Jinping from resorting to a force of arms. Why is this critical? Because when President Jinping finds himself unable to control the outrage he created internationally he will claim false flag operations. This will create confusion and further induce extremists to counter the United States militarily. This chaos, if allowed to spread, will allow Xi Jinping to characterize the West as weak. From this perspective President Jinping would have nothing to lose by catalyzing frustration. The only solution is to isolate him legally and economically, ideally within the closed confines of the markets President Jinping relies upon to generate reserve currencies. The US will need to reassure the public that America remains ready to re-engage with China and that alternate markets remain secure, while emphasizing that President Jinping is fomenting instability internationally. The focus needs to remain narrowly directed at Xi Jinping as a man who has lost control over himself and his Party.

The sense of alienation that President Jinping generates regarding China's position with the rest of the world is what he uses to set the stage for militarism. Extreme passion of purpose achieves balance only through the release of action. The threat of violence is what Xi Jinping uses to keep his foreign opponents off balance. He portrays the US as incompetent, and if his followers erupt in denunciations of the United States this only means that America is at fault for unfairly asserting its position as the World largest economy. This will become a contradictory and difficult dilemma for Trump to counter, both as a potential Chinese antagonist and trading partner. More work must be done from a legal perspective internationally to publicly emphasize that the monitoring of extremists in China is ongoing, and that militarism will not be tolerated.

President Jinping's pronouncements of manipulation by the international order needs to be delegitimized in an easily digested assessment of the entire international system where forceful refutations of President Jinping's ongoing efforts to discredit America must be routinized.

Ask for public comment in China unfettered by censors. This will deflate the bubble. Demonstrate that the fragmented nature of the international system also renders it less vulnerable to manipulation. Highlight that Chinese Communist attempts to restrict the discussion expends copious amounts of energy in an attempt to defend the indefensible. Let them. The louder President Jinping decries this process, the closer he will be to being disbelieved.

Lastly actively reveal President Jinping's sources of financial influence. The Communist Party remains vulnerable here, so this will need to be countered with entreaties and proposals for reform. Connect financial support to income stratification in China. Connect corruption to increasing incidents of violence. Associate this to Communist Party representatives in affected districts who have been endorsed by President Jinping. Care must be taken to keep the focus on those with a direct connection to the President. Use this to highlight the hypocrisy of the Communist the Party as a way to shine a light on a deeply compromised Jinping government.

To President Jinping's devotees it does not matter that he lacks coherence, only that they can join a cause that is focused on one man. President Jinping is not a fanatic. His commitment is both narcissistic and nationalistic. As China's new Son of Heaven (Tianzi), there is no distinction in him from any other Emperor, King, Czar, Fuhrer, or Paramount Leader. They are all the same.

President Jinping's exhortation is to reject American hegemony, and he implies that United States intends to enable the tyranny of a minority over a Sino majority. Narrowly describing the US as a Christian imposition of a Nationalistic ideal on the rest of world allows the entire United States to be stereotyped and described as a culture that can only be countered by force. This is one of many reasons why the Evangelical movement in the United States is so dangerous. Asia does not share this perspective of the world, and Trump, ironically a faithless non-believer, has already been forced to adopt it. President Jinping, even if he wanted to prevent violence of action in response to what he perceives, not unjustifiably, as an inflexible perspective on humanity, could not prevent it. It will happen.

THE SUM OF ZERO 饮水思源

8

President Jinping's impact on the military must now be considered in terms of his arrogance if he chooses to initiate a strategy centered on a force of arms. War is never humbly initiated. It fails to recognize that importance of the individual and undervalues human life. It contains within it many similarities to a mass movement and as such is also an instrument of coercion. The military also offers refuge for those who feel directionless. It also provides opportunities for the ambitious. It is a mechanism of unquestioning routine and as such offers President Jinping many options for consolidating and maintaining control. It will not matter to the military rank and file that they defend a Chinese Peoples Republic or Autocratic Presidency. Military leadership that balks at the idea of a Commander in Chief who is not encumbered by checks and balances will be replaced. Even jailed.

One does not need to wonder at the probability of such an event. Threatened he will implement it. Implemented he will turn China into a military dictatorship, and as an Autocrat he will maintain his grip on the Presidency beyond the scope of his competency as a leader. This will be done within the framework of an emergency. An emergency that he will fabricate and create by unleashing the military on a global scapegoat. Undoubtedly it will start small but grow in scope. History is rife with examples of near-term military successes that turn into long-term autocratic nightmares. The victim will be world peace and Chinese prosperity. Once the ball starts rolling, however unintentionally, President Jinping will not be able to stop it. The world will unite against him. He is not omniscient nor omnipotent. He needs to be considered within a framework of impulsive and incurious self-indulgence. The Communist Party needs to be awakened to the fact that President Jinping is a clear and present danger for China and for the World.

Why the West does not express continual outrage and place the blame aggressively on President Jinping is an act of cowardice. They are complicit to the extent that they permit trade relations to purchase foreign policy. President Jinping is a product of a zero-sum perspective of politics, and the United States will continue to be at risk as long as it is so.

America is already paralyzed by the influence of money in politics that parades as a service to the Nation. America's representative democracy is an embarrassment, but that does not mean it will be permanently disgraced by a figurehead who is a traitor, draft dodger, and convicted felon. China on the other hand accepts a leader who cannot be removed. He represents a far greater danger to his nation than the orange clown currently chosen by an imperfect representative democracy in America.

It is President Jinping's hatred of those he feels ridicule his bloated conception of Chinese Communist self-actualization that generates his disdain for American politics. His contempt provides him with his excuse for violence. President Jinping metastasizes his narcissism in an impression of himself as possessing a mandate that only he can fulfill – the most dangerous kind of demagogue. Render him a ridiculous pretender, as a man who playacts at a Confucian definition of leadership that is based on respect and trust, that assumes a wise leader will avoid violence, that they will be humble and open to feedback from others, and that they will strive for balance and avoid the extremes of conceit.

Fear breeds hate. Want breeds fear. When you realize something you want badly is beyond your grasp your fear turns to hate, and hate is the most powerful of all emotions because Hate can be easily rationalized by Pride, the deadliest of all sins because it is used to rationalize all of the others.

Pride is an excessive love of self. Taken to an extreme it is a loss of respect for your neighbor. Pride involves an inflated sense of self-importance, an excessive focus on oneself, and a failure to acknowledge one's dependence on God. With humility comes wisdom. With Pride comes ignorance, greed, lust, envy, and gluttony. Pride always presages violence and destruction. Overconfident and condescending arrogance uses this to justify otherwise criminal and immoral actions. It is the bane of every Populist. These are the qualities exhibited by President Jinping and President Trump, characteristics that render them singularly unfit for office.

President Jinping is a textbook case on Fear and Pride. At his core he feels himself superior, and when he perceives that his goals are at risk he allows anger to dominate his emotions, which are then followed by threats of vengeance and violence. Because President Jinping has a warped perception of self he redefines his opponents as enemies in order to justify his Pride.

His claims that America is weaponizing his opponents is irrelevant. He has to make extreme claims in order to create an identifiable target from which he can inculcate a belief of intractable corruption in the United States. The hate he foments is not optional for him, but this also presents President Jinping with a dilemma. Trump may be insulting and unlikable, but America is not uncaring and callous, and even though President Jinping keeps up a continuous barrage of inuendo, lies, and insults, these bullying tactics, while at times entertaining, appear immature and desperate.

All the United States needs to do to counter this is to continue to demonstrate discernable acts of empathy and support for those who are distressed in China. Marketable events of empathy combined with clear analysis and proposals for continued progress that underscore the appreciation America has for the Chinese cultural experience will dilute Jinping's legitimacy. President Jinping is incapable of doing the same. Otherwise he would lose his appeal as a sanctified Paramount Leader. The differences would be stark, and the advantage would accrue to Trump.

An interesting corollary regarding how to undermine President Jinping would need to be designed to challenge the single-issue focus of his base – how to assure access to opportunity by complying with communist doctrine as defined by President Jinping. Continue to sow doubt – in the man. This loosens the hold President Jinping has on his supporters, which needs to be supplemented with demonstrative actions that the West holds a high regard for China's citizens, while harboring a genuine concern for wisdom of its President.

Trump needs to describe President Jinping as a loathsome figure against whom a defeat can be seen as a triumph over corruption and a win for Chinese prosperity.

Associate this with a focus on President Jinping's foreign entanglements, and the support he provides Putin and Kim. Attaching President Jinping's lapses in judgement to his public statements is what is needed to blunt the impact of his attacks on the United States. Demonstrate that they are the product of a disturbed mind. It must not be a refutation of President Jinping's lie, because his lies hold no basis in fact. Instead what needs to be shown is that these statements are designed to purposefully mislead and generate fear and hate. Show that President Jinping's inane invectives are the product of a deeply misguided Communist perspective that lacks discipline and a regard for common sense.

President Jinping is irrational. His grievances lack a basis in fact and revolve around half-truths. His gripes are childish, and in this way he demonstrates that he desperately wants to be acknowledged. Ironically, the praise he levels on Putin, while staggering in what it implies, is understandable when one considers how isolated he must feel. He strives to convert the inadequacy and failings of his own government into a hate of outside influences. President Jinping feels a natural affinity for leaders isolated by America. Do not doubt that he desires to impose this kind of isolation on the American political system as well.

President Jinping imagines an intense hatred for any truth that denunciates him and convinces him of his many weaknesses. Xi Jinping is a deeply insecure man, and it is this aspect of his personality that leads him to self-justify. He is sanctimonious because he needs to be. His desire to deride and injure his opponents also is a form of self-justification, an attitude that he attempts to inculcate in his followers. This anger and hate only breeds more contempt within him, which he uses to rationalize a call to violence. From this perspective President Jinping will soon lose control over the emotions he has unleashed. He will have set in motion an intense desire to reject external influences on Chinese culture. This Hate will breed a shamelessness that will render those wracked by it impervious to criticism and argument.

Hate has a strange association with jealousy. Those whom we feel are our betters are far easier to despise than those for whom we feel pity. President Jinping feels that Trump is his inferior but knows that Trump feels he is the Teacher. Privately Xi ridicules and wonders at the immaturity and ignorance of the man.

China has long felt itself to be the greatest of nations. This places China in the unique position of looking inward when comparing itself to others. This creates in China a tension that is exacerbated by an impression of American privilege, all the more conflicting because in some sense America is deserving of its prosperity.

As Americans begin to lose faith in the American dream, they will also begin to turn their gaze inward in an attempt to focus external blame. Others, China in particular, will be attributed to be the source of many of their difficulties. What makes the Trump trope unique is that will he attach this to an idea of conspiracy manipulating population as subterfuge designed to affect a long-term diminution of the influence enjoyed by the United States. In this way he will further exacerbate the idea that American promise and privilege is being stolen from a deserving working-class citizen by a conniving Chinese President. He would not be wrong in this assumption. It is an overt and defining element of President Jinping's long-term strategy - to supplant, dominate, and replace the United States as this plant's pre-eminent nation.

In President Jinping there is a kind of veneration of the United States. He spent time here, admires America, and in berating the United States as committing the basest forms of political manipulation, he carries out the same. He claims he is countering political perversion, not because he believes our system is corrupt, but because he is attempting to provoke. This has the effect of transforming those who oppose President Jinping into doppelgangers. In this way political diplomacy as a whole is weakened and demeaned, providing a further confirmation that President Jinping is a dangerous promoter of international confrontation.

Hate has no boundaries and flows to where it can be most effective and where opposition is weak. The hostility Xi Jinping creates provides his diplomacy a momentum that propels the Nation towards what he hopes will be a check on American hegemony. This is a dangerous game, and already takes on the form of low-grade aggression. Do not doubt that violence will happen when it involves a China that feels aggrieved historically. The initial flash point will happen in the China Sea, and eventually lead to a blockade of Taiwan. A high seas confrontation is inevitable and at some point we will see the first use of a low yield nuclear weapon against a US naval squadron in international waters. Trade with China will cease. The planet will regionalize, and stalemate will settle over the Pacific. Wars are not won by strategy. They are won by attrition. Taiwan will be lost, but this will be the beginning of the end for President Jinping as he confronts the productive capability of a world arrayed against him. The only question that will remain is whether the transition in China result in a more aggressively belligerent regime, or a return to Chinese entente.

Xi Jinping's mistake is that international intransigence will severely damage China. China needs the world, and the world needs China. If China is injured economically, it will have the potential to cause coordinated civil disobedience that begins to disperse across the nation. It will presage the beginning of the end for President Jinping. His regime seems incapable of compromise and will consume the political capital of those around it. If internal conflicts spreads, he will use it as an excuse to purge his ranks and invest in an automated surveillance society. He will promote militarism. Indeed he already started this process, which as mentioned above, will allow him to quash dissent at the level of the individual. To the degree he is able to implement this program of control he will then have the wherewithal to turn China into an Orwellian reality. Do not doubt that this will happen in a nation where there is already a complete lack of privacy and dearth of personal choice. For President Jinping the power provided by an automated AI based surveillance society will be impossible to resist.

President Jinping's regime does not simply want to change the direction of the nation, they also want to humiliate their opponents. Hence his program of vengeance. He will start by disarming internal opposition, never mind that innovators such as Jack Ma are the wealth creation engine of the nation. If President Jinping feels hindered, he will legally find a way to apply his will by force. To this end he will enlist pliable elements of the military that he will activate immediately if he feels threatened. Unquestioning loyalty will become more important to him than mandates set down as devotion to principle. Once this autocracy fully metastasizes in Beijing, the result will be a society of severe punishments and absolute obeisance.

President Jinping is Chauvinistic, and this causes him to be cruel and unsympathetic. His immodesty also breeds a conceit and a disdain for others. This leads him to condescension and arrogance. Because President Jinping sees himself as self-realized and even necessary, he considers himself absolved of responsibility.

Freed from responsibility for his actions he will become callous, and provide himself with the authority to intimidate, lie, betray, and even torture, without shame or compunction. His hatred will become self-reinforcing. He has already shamelessly perverted the Communist ideal of governance. He debases Chinese dissention as if it were a sin in order to create an impression that he is a capable leader. His personification of a depraved spirituality is an example of his ongoing attempt to redefine Communism into a personal mandate.

President Jinping's campaign is political Simon Says. His supporters are forced to interpret commands that could be genuine but also might be fake. President Jinping uses this to inculcate acquiescence in his followers while instilling in them an imprecation to follow. He does this by imposing a requirement of unquestioning loyalty, but what he is really doing is asking others to mimic his behavior in order to foster obedience. This also insulates his followers from outside influences. This creates in them a false confidence that cements them to his cause. This assurance also breeds in them a feeling that they are superior, which then further motivates them to emulate their leader – a man who provides them with a sense that they have value and purpose. This is what makes Xi Jinping's base so resilient.

Homogeneity breeds uniformity. Uniformity breeds a contempt for external influences and so constitutes another reason why President Jinping's base is so cohesive. It is an innate defiance that further isolates China. It does not matter what Xi Jinping's message is, only that he appears to talk directly to his supporters as members of the elect.

Rendering President Jinping's persona laughable, embarrassing, and pathetic is what is needed to break the populous free from this indoctrination. When an imitation of him no longer offers reward for a revised sense of self, President Jinping's supporters will once again develop an impression that they are isolated, alone, and forgotten. This is when they will be at their most vulnerable and receptive to the welcoming proposals of a new cause.

As their dedication to the man becomes increasingly indecisive, the cohesiveness of his base will become brittle, and as such susceptible to ideas that confuse, disassociate, disorder, scatter and garble the visuals of President Jinping's message. Visuals which center on the character of the man himself. Left disoriented President Jinping's devotees will be at their most receptive to messages that refocus their attention on a new and more worthy mandate.

President Jinping's supporters are willfully uninformed. They are not inclined to research and confirm his character and policy. In fact it would be a waste of their time to do so. In this way all of China is politically immature, and highly vulnerable to freelance authorities. This becomes all the more pronounced in those individuals who strive to escape from a conception of self in which they believe themselves to be personal failures deserving of condemnation. Because the Jinping adherent is willfully incurious, and lacks access to informational resources, they can be easily deceived, and this constitutes both a strength and weakness for the President. This is why Xi Jinping uses a heavy hand to isolate China. It is the disrespect and hate he breeds for external influences that separates his nation from the rest of the world, which is why the United States must work to generate contempt for the Man, not his policies.

SMALL FRY 治大国若烹小鲜

9

President Jinping is neither a great communicator nor syllogist. He is instead a distorted publicist. And because he is a propagandist he does not so much convince as force his opinions upon people. They have no choice but to 'believe'. To do otherwise would expose them to the disenfranchising vulnerabilities of government sanctioned surveillance. This peculiar form of confirmation bias is what President Jinping uses to manipulate, his supporters imagining that cabals are working to suppress them in order to coopt otherwise enlightened perspectives.

President Jinping is herding his believers towards a belief that violence will be a requisite step in his bid to restore China. Legalized terror is what will spring from this chrysalis of intolerance. Do not doubt that this will happen in a nation that has still uses concentration camps to suppress dissent.

President Jinping's style of proselytizing is coercive, and as his military approaches an inflection point of parity we will find that his intellectual conceit finds ever more ways to ignore bias and rationalize motivation. There will come a time when the personal corruption of President Jinping the man, President Jinping the Manager, and his status as a Communist Pretender, is rationalized by a self-serving intellectual elite in the name of countering all sides of the arguments against him. Taken to an extreme it will be used to absolve the man of his actions. After all when does leadership and the necessity for making 'hard choices' devolve into criminality. When looked at from an ethical perspective, for any leader there is often a regression into questionable proclivities. When these acts are isolated and looked at in the bright light of what is right and wrong, these actions are simply crimes, often magnified into offenses against humanity. This is the great danger inherent in any autocracy, an unfortunate characteristic that is imbedded in a President Jinping regime legitimized by the Paramount Leaders who came before him.

In China ignorance is not incompatible with intellect, although to be blunt this is the often the case for many accomplished Intellectuals, likely the result of the rationalizing power of Pride. For many in China, this will be a simple act of pusillanimity born from selfishness, jealousy, and greed, rationalized as a meritorious example of intellectual loyalty.

President Jinping presages the use of power in the service of a maintenance of presidential tenure. The burgeoning militancy of the nation has also embraced this idea of a militarized Marxism. From each according to his ability and to each according their Guns is needed to excise what is described as a rot in International Politics, beginning with the expulsion of those who have poisoned the cultural sanctity of what was once a great Chinese oriental hegemony organized under the mandate of Sino Manifest Destiny.

President Jinping perceives that preventing Chinese subordination is inextricably linked to the elevation of himself as an unassailable champion of the Chinese Communist Cause. In this way it is critical that the West portray Jinping as the Great Deceiver who would bind and blind men to his will. Use of fascist characterizations is unseemly, and must be used with care, but must be done. President Jinping can be damaged by using images that instill a fear in China about his intent. Civil war is always just around the corner in a stifled Communist China.

The outrageous nature of President Jinping's message has its roots in his rural upbringing. This though has been put at risk as China has stratified privilege, which is now perceived as being under increasing threat from the diluting impact of intra-national migration. It is this perceived loss of advantage that drives President Jinping to tighten his grip. The flip side of party affiliation is privilege. Privilege in China is also often racist. President Jinping recognizes this but has transformed it into an excuse to eradicate the cultural identity of Uyghurs, ethnic Kazakhs and Kyrgyz, and members of religious minority groups – rooted in a suppression of the idea of liberty in favor of a homogenous and intolerant Nationalist Chinese communist experience.

What is the character of the Populist? They are aggressive, instinctive, driven, purposeful, and certain about their instincts, but they are also dissolute, profligate, immoral, disgraceful, impious, and dissipated. Does this describe President Jinping?

Every age contains its own peculiar flavor of fascism. Self-appointed Emperors, Party Chairmen, and Presidents for Life all revolve around the idea of an infallible leader, and in this President Jinping is no exception. This type of narcissist gains popularity not from a belief that they represent the best of citizenship, but instead arises from a deep discontent with the current state of affairs in politics and government. Without this sense of frustration this type of Leader becomes nothing more than an immodest activist and blowhard.

The disgrace of British Imperialism and the Opium Wars laid the foundation for the fragmentation of Chinese Society and opened the path for the fascist invasion of China by a militarized Japan. Chiang Kai-shek then necessarily spent the Chinese capacity for political cohesiveness in fighting the invader, which then rendered China unable to fight off the political infection that was Mao.

This inward focus has distracted China from pressing social issues and reallocated resources to unattributable benefits based on irrational communist principles, which has, as is the case in the Soviet Union, eventually centered around internal policing and investments in military capability to fend off imagined foreign threats. No advantage accrued to China during this initial transition to a centralized economy, a travesty that turned into tragedy on an unimaginable scale, and what has provided the basis for the creation of the cartoon parody of communism that is President Jinping. In this way he is an accident of the Chinese Communist political experience.

To remove him from the stage will require refocusing attention on the needs and priorities of the Chinese populous, starting with an emphasis on principles of prosperity and self-determination.

President Jinping is not a man of unrivaled intelligence. What he is a man who lives behind a façade of a cult of personality, who is capable of legitimizing hate with a stunning disregard for precepts of propriety. It might be suggested that he has a calculating insight into human nature, but this proclivity to label him a political savant is far too generous an accolade for a man of such limited discernment. Inarticulate grandeur combined with irreverent certitude is what President Jinping uses to replace the petty meanness that exists in his supporters with a sureness of purpose. He is riding a wave of nationalistic pride to which he attaches his own peculiar flaws of character. He is a man of the moment and will soon find a ready font of hubris contained within the flattery of those who humor him. That is until they find they can rid themselves of their resentment of his influence.

President Jinping's policies have yet to gestate into a form of overt fascism, but he is moving inexorably in that direction. An indication that he has arrived will be when he adopts a new symbol peculiar to his regime. At that point he will have transformed himself into a heroic lampoon of the Communist experience, which will indicate that he intends to subvert Marxist principles and implement a tyranny of the minority in the name of strengthening the Peoples Republic.

The shame of his lieutenants is that they have allowed themselves to be spellbound by an image of a great leader who will in the end destroy them all. An attempt must be made to convert their cowardice into a fear that they will ultimately be sacrificed on President Jinping's altar of loyalty. They have within them an infuriated resentment of the man, which can be used to sow doubt about Xi Jinping's character.

What President Jinping does seem to have is a capacity for white washing outrageous directives with a bland disregard for convention. And while previous 20th century populists exhibited fanaticism, this characteristic in President Jinping looks to be a slavish commitment to a narrow-minded ignorance and his own inflated sense of self-worth. The man is so offensively pre-packaged that he must be made to seem ridiculous in his follower's eyes. He is a Brand, and an example of hubris who will resort to violence if it serves his purpose.

One of the more surprising manifestations of President Jinping's style of leadership is the stoicism of his character, and the featureless content of his remarks. Because of the preposterous illogic of his ideas he must pronounce them with absolute certainty. He must convey his ideas with unrestrained self-assurance, because what is important to his supporters is the big-headed grand gesture, the contempt he has for the opinion of others, and his defiance of superior evidence to contrary. They use this to rid themselves of the idea that they themselves are devoid of original thinking.

President Jinping knows that he is an imposter. All Communists are, but in some ways this is central to the marketing of the brand. His supporters require of him a methodical twisting of the facts. And this is also why President Jinping gaslights, accusing his opponents so blatantly of those very same things he is guilty of. He calls the US Administration a disgrace, which at times it has been, because he has frequently and publicly been accused of the same. In a way even to himself he is without definition. He is a shell that he fills with reactive misrepresentations of reality so that he can shield himself from irrelevance.

His diatribes make no sense, and because they have no basis in fact they cannot be assailed with fact. The only response that can be used to counter his frequently inane comments is that they are untrue, that they are lies, and that there is no evidence that these accusations exist in reality. At that point the argument simply trails off into incredulity, while President Jinping is left with the bulk of his statements intact. This is why the man himself, not his argument must be attacked. To the extent his image is weakened, his misrepresentations will begin to destabilize. President Jinping is an incongruity of alternate facts. These contradictions infuse his personality and as such leave him singularly vulnerable to character deconstruction. Market his personality as an incredulous exposé on the vacuous nature of the man himself. The connection he has to his policies will then immediately begin to fray.

President Jinping's followers find relief in the ease with which they relinquish independent thought. They are insecure and so have an innate inclination to follow. For President Jinping's admirers, freedom and liberty are attained in the equality of their position as one of his followers. Satisfaction is derived for them in the shouldering of a collective enterprise. This is why if President Jinping fails, his followers will blankly stare back at any accusation that they are also to blame, because in their minds it was a politicized endeavor for which they shoulder no individual culpability. For this reason they will be eager to follow the next cause with no sense of shame regarding the previous. It is counterproductive and makes no sense to accuse Jinping's supporters. They subsume responsibility to President Jinping himself. It is of no importance to them what he does, only that they are being led by him. Their sacrifice without recompense will be Xi Jinping's reward.

What is the main area of difference between Deng Xiaoping and President Jinping as leaders? Deng Xiaoping believed he had a responsibility to unleash the creative spirit and wisdom of the Chinese political collective in support of a mandate to support the nation in its pursuit of prosperity and happiness. President Jinping on the other hand believes some must suffer in favor of those who support Party policy. He believes that all men will ultimately pursue what is best for them in abeyance of what is needed for the many. His vision requires that a proportionate allocation of rewards goes to the most deserving, and that this depends on an obedience to his cause. This is a concept that holds that all men when left to their own designs will ultimately pursue what is best for them regardless of the impact it has on others. Do not doubt that President Jinping has adopted this perspective of humanity. He is an aberrant narcissist and as such feels that he is the most deserving of all. He will be rapacious in his pursuit of accolades, power, and the installation of a dynasty that is tasked with maintaining what in his mind is a pre-destined event based on the force of his will alone.

The Tiananmen Massacre was not a random event. While President Jinping does not intend to repeat this tragedy, he is working to prevent that necessity through targeted control and surveillance of the populous at the community level. This is an inevitable consequence of his need to maintain a focus on him as a figurehead and leader. This is because his call to conform acts to solidify and reconfirm a commitment to him as a Populist. If President Jinping had not initiated this call to adhere to party policy his base would fracture, and he would not be the unopposed Paramount Leander he is today. This is why it is inevitable that he will resort to an inducement to violence as an action external to the Republic. It is a requisite part of the process of any Populist that is needed to maintain commitment. For President Jinping's believers this call to action creates within them a comfortable comradeship, one that allows them to lose themselves within a cause they perceive is greater than themselves.

It must be remembered that the intractable dilemma of Chinese politics is the apathy of its citizens that reveals itself in a resignation that the State frees them from the burden of choice, but also relieves them from personal responsibility. The current effect is that they demonstrate greater enthusiasm for privileges of party membership than for the promises offered by self-determination. The West needs to shake them out of their apathy by fomenting disgust for President Jinping. Attach the worst of what China is to President Jinping's regime. Provide endless examples of social injustice, party corruption, and unequal health care, where Chinese obesity already consumes 1/5th of the health care budget. And of bankruptcies caused by party policy where workers lose everything in unpredictable markets. Demonstrate that this is all done within a framework that allows the wealthy endless opportunities to escape their obligations to the Nation.

It will be easy to attach this to Communist policies. Hammer home that the Party uses its offices to enrich itself. Attach them aggressively to favors which they sell to others. Do more than simply provide numeric illustrations of abuse. Attach visuals to examples of their wealth accumulation in terms of houses, boats, planes, and the like. Associate abuses of the Chinese fiscal system to the manipulation of foreign investment, government sponsored industries, and investments in infrastructure. President Jinping's supporters know only a little of this and will feel abused. Demonstrate that far from desiring to change the system for the better, his goal is to maintain power and systematically abuse the system for his own benefit.

The United States must create an idea of President Jinping as a noxious miasma of overlooked corruption. Demonstrate that the Communist Party focus is not on people but on the maintenance of privilege. Hold up a corrupted Politburo as an example of a misuse of power that goes all the way to the top. Show that the time has arrived to roll out term limit proposals for Presidents and Paramount Leaders alike. Propose impeachment mechanisms for the removal of corrupt Chinese leaders from office. President Jinping is an unrestrained autocrat. Until this changes all of China, and indeed the world, will be at risk.

President Jinping's supporters at times appear to be intransigent and invulnerable, but in actuality to the extent they perceive themselves to be successful agents of change, they carry within them the seeds of destruction for President Jinping and his regime. It will not be enough for detractors to say that Xi Jinping, the Communist Party, and his coopted Politburo are corrupt. Visual examples of their graft must be attached to them even as they attempt to portray themselves as sacrificing in the name of service to Country. The target here is the vacuous average Chinese citizen who can still be shown that they are in reality dismissed and reviled. Demonstrate that constraints on power and openness in foreign policy are what offers them their only real opportunity for salvation.

President Jinping's beneficiaries are overwhelmed by fear. Their self-abasement manifests itself in the apprehension they hold for others outside of the Party. Xi Jinping uses this to keep his supporters and acolytes in a continual state of anxiety about their position within his hierarchy. His disparagement of Party detractors creates fear and isolates critical appraisals of policy. The intent is to offer them up as a sacrifice to the cause in order to keep apprehension at a fever pitch. The goal is to maintain unquestioning loyalty to an idea that is President Jinping.

Divisiveness brought about by an abandonment of principles is what further isolates the Jinping enthusiast. This is dangerous because it provides a foundation for an acceleration of hate, and in this way President Jinping's beneficiaries become even more extreme in their commitment. As the intensity of their commitment increases, the loathing they feel for Western Democracies, and in particular America, will increase, to the point where their acceptance of alternate systems of governance become unsustainable – a prelude to violence.

When this occurs the average Chinese citizen will have completely surrendered their power of choice or any inclination to disagree, even privately, with the man himself. They will feel as if they have been provided dispensation from the vagaries of an otherwise unstable political system. They will then latch on to a President Jinping program of racial superiority and work to silence dissent. When this happens they will be used to transform the nation into a militaristic champion for an imperial Chinese Autocracy.

The wasting of an enlightened intellectual Chinese lexicon is the real tragedy of President Jinping. His is a perversion of principles. But if the Chinese Communist experiment has been polluted it is because of the corrupting influence of money in Communism. President Jinping is a tumor that springs from this. If not him, it would have been someone else.

President Jinping's cruelty is a form of sanctioned coercion, and he must as a matter of course discredit the US system of jurisprudence in order to break China's connection to the US as a desirable alternative. To the extent that he can maintain a faith in Chinese institutions, and reframe change as modernization, the public will be less receptive to a radical rejection of President Jinping's policies. The West must describe Jinping as duplicitous, dangerous, and even delusional. The danger here is that this will induce him to react violently, but if this can be contained it will weaken his government. It could even be desirable in that it would prompt a deviant response so severe that he could be made to seem faithless to the Chinese Nationalist ideal.

An associated danger for Western Democracies is that Jinping effectively utilizes compromised men of action to provide momentum for his policies. Connect the man to these delegitimizers and demonstrate that they are themselves compromised. That they are men and women who associate themselves with a Communist parody in an attempt to gain power and accumulate wealth. Show the Chinese public that they exist apart from China as a privileged and corrupted element of the party. A Party that has prostituted its ethics to a man without integrity, conscience, or morals.

Furthermore the United States must work to separate an expressive subgroup of Jinping supporters from the whole. This segment of the Communist Party needs an excuse to redirect support. Induce this via tangible examples of immoderate policies followed by an acknowledgement that these policies are not sustainable. Case in point, a fully, not partially, and equitably funded education and health care system. No restricted access to services. This needs to be portrayed as a purposeful perspective of the Party. An intentional abandonment of the average Chinese citizen.

The United States could even acknowledge that President Jinping was right in stating that tariffs injure both nations. Tariffs are half court tennis. What Trump fails to consider is that there are 2 sides and another player on the court. (A metaphor used by Historian Sarah Paine) As an example, in 1930 the US passed Smoot-Hawley Tariff Act to protect US jobs and manufacturing. A devastating 6 year worldwide depression occurred because of this decision. What was not anticipated was the affect this would have on Japan, which was restricted from trading with the US. Japan then looked to Imperialism as an alternative. 1 year after passage of the Act Japan would attack Manchuria, and the rest is history. Life (and international trade) is an interaction. A conciliatory gesture from Trump that does not reference Xi but instead takes in to account the affects tariffs will have on American and Chinese demographics could win many over to his side, and importantly weaken Xi. We need to remember that China craves recognition and respect. Acknowledge China's concerns while rejecting President

Jinping as a man who is lamentable and unworthy of imitation. Emotionally connect a Jinping Presidency to the certainty that China will suffer as he redirects his support to Putin, Kim, and Iran. Portray Ukraine's struggle as one that bears similarities to Taiwan's struggle for self-determination. Use this to demonstrate that President Jinping is a political perversion who needs to be prevented from moving China away from a productive relationship with the United States and the World.

Xi Jinping yearns for prestige and adulation. His vanity drives him to crave a constant reconfirmation of this status, which is what drove him to politics in the first place. What we need to remember is that he takes criticism personally. If he feels disrespected, this stimulates his baser emotions.

President Jinping has earned an indulgence far beyond the breadth of his abilities as a politician. It is distressing to see the praise some intellectuals heap upon a man of such limited insight. They throw accolades at him in the hope that he will grant them dispensations. Instead, what they will find is that their loyalty will be revealed as pedantic and unappreciated.

Xi Jinping warps the Chinese myth. America needs to create a restored faith and admiration in a Western perspective of Chinese greatness. At a minimum it will confuse President Jinping's supporters who gravitate naturally to such ideas. At its best it will reveal the President to be a propagandist who is more interested in misleading than leading. Ignorance can never be discredited, only rendered laughable and worthy of derision.

The West needs to remember that the humiliations heaped on the Chinese are real and that they need to be addressed with concrete diplomatic reconciliations. The concerns of a population that gravitates to an autocrat have real apprehensions that must not be overlooked in the push and pull of media influencers who favor a prioritization of the President's concerns, versus the imbalances caused by Chinese domestic and international policies.

What President Jinping is doing is laying the groundwork for a China that is expressly less tolerant. He has started by discrediting what he references as anti-Chinese ethnicities. He sets China adrift by creating doubt and then offers himself up as a life raft for the disillusioned. He bolsters his promises with slogans and a code of belief that perverts the Communist ideal

Already his opposition has lost the will to resist him. Western democracies hope that the priorities of a Chinese export driven economy will be able to rein in Jinping but will find that he has already subsumed this imperative to the office of the Presidency. A new order has already been imposed on China's relationship with world. What Xi Jinping will do is let loose a process that will impose a system of intransigence and confrontation in international relations. Jinping will not care. By then his vision of a Pacific region dominated by China will have succeeded him.

It needs to be remembered that Xi Jinping's base wants to abrogate their authority to a one-party solution led by a one-man structure. They do not crave individual freedoms, but instead want to align themselves with a homogeneity of purpose that will rise against what they perceive as weakness in fragmented systems of government. The US must counter this with authoritative pronouncements that demonstrate the US can exercise economic and moral authority when appropriate and when required. Do this within a recognition that it is the Chinese experience that must be respected by revising the strictures defined by communist orthodoxy.

THE SNAKE HAS LEGS 画蛇添足

10

Let us call them what they are. Incomprehensible idiots, the lot of them, starting with many of the inane Communist Representatives in the Politburo. They accept a President Jinping program that uses the irrational to imply that he has clarity of purpose. President Jinping has added to otherwise laudable Communist principles of community, capitalist appendages that he uses to reinforce the idea that he is a leader propitiously positioned at just the right time to bring order to the nation. What he has done instead is overlay equality with iniquity.

Xi Jinping appears to be man with a singular deficit in his capacity for inquisitiveness. When you combine this with his odd inability to experience empathy, you find in Xi Jinping a man who is singularly incurious. Pair this with an extreme narcissism and it renders him exceptionally unfit to lead the Chinese nation. What his narcissism does do is arm him with a peculiar capacity for accusation and condemnation, two qualities that do not require much in the area of contemplative thought. An interesting corollary is that his supporters desire the same – a program of dissent that does not require much in the way self-reflection. It is a way for them to avoid a confirmation that they are worthy of condemnation.

Another interesting aspect of Xi Jinping's burgeoning hold on the Party is that his extremes have begun to create cracks in the party framework. Dissention has already begun to infect the ranks. His supporters make enemies of one another, which drives them to extremes in their attempt to align themselves with the President. This only serves to further destabilize the message and purpose that President Jinping will need to convey in order maintain his office. And while it is unlikely that his support will meaningfully drain away, the hold he wishes to maintain on his position will weaken. The more tightly he tries to control his message the more irrational it will become, which is precisely what is needed to be emphasized to loosen his grip on power.

President Jinping's greatest vulnerability is President Jinping himself. He will inevitably get in his own way. His pronouncements attempt to be practical but are in actuality illogical and extreme. The directness of his observations though can at times be surprisingly prescient. The US does need to acknowledge that the Chinese political experience has validity even though it is not conducive to democratic plurality.

This does not mean though that the majority of Xi Jinping's policies are appropriate. It is not OK if Putin attacks Ukraine. Deporting ethnic undesirables is not moral. Denying Tibet autonomy is a travesty. Rejecting Taiwanese self-determination is Imperialism. His statements bely an undisciplined mind that is both impulsive and irrational, which presages that his policies will become increasingly erratic. Use it against him. Unfortunately, his intransigent management style also makes him unpredictability dangerous. He lacks a capacity for re-evaluation and compromise, and if he continues in office his actions will almost certainly begin a dismantling of China's complementary integration with the world.

President Jinping's preoccupation is not to cooperatively reinvent China's relationship with the world but to acquire it. His goals will turn to prolonging and consolidating his hold on power. At first to deflect attempts to weaken his position, the result will be rules that make his removal more difficult. In this way he will have created a de-facto Chinese Kingship. Mao's lifetime tenure is already being repeated and the dynamism of the Chinese cultural experience will be neutered. Do not doubt that President Jinping will attempt to do this, he has already begun its enfranchisement.

The constitutional oath of office of China was implemented on January 1, 2016. If President Jinping attempts to insert himself into the pledge in order crystalize loyalty we will know that he intends to replace communist institutions with a new President Jinping cult of personality. If he supplements this with a personal symbol, we can be assured that he is attempting to replicate the excesses of National Socialism. And finally, if this is realized via a AI managed consolidation and compromise of the nation's traditional administrative structures, China will be turned into an oligarchic kleptocracy.

We will see greed and ambition crystallize around this President beginning with his personal and family fortune. The meek will be disinherited and rendered inconsequential within a new Chinese political framework.

What will be of interest is whether President Jinping finds that he needs to turn to the Military to maintain social control. If dissent spirals out of control, he will either manufacture or escalate a local crisis as a means of deflecting attention away from the failings of his office. When he does this he will invoke a national imperative that infuses Communism in a semi-religious obligation to restore order. He will manufacture an excuse that requires him to impose emergency powers that mobilize the military. Interestingly a medical pandemic would serve this purpose admirably. Internationally an expanded Airforce and Navy supplemented with overseas port and airbases which could then be used to cover major trade routes would also accomplish this goal of focusing Chinese discontent away from internal challenges.

President Jinping's administration is destined to be unpleasant and demoralizing. He will be callous and smug. He will be ready to sacrifice his comrades if necessary to maintain his hold on power, and in the process will sacrifice Chinese institutions in his desire to consolidate control. Indeed he has already done so with Chinese academia.

President Jinping's legacy will be a period of stagnation and inflated prices as he wastes China's comparative advantage in technology and labor. He will turn the levers of the IT age into mechanisms of surveillance, and from there implement control in the name of security and compliance with rule of law. Investments in infrastructure will be transformed into projects of militarized vanity. Communist party safety nets such as they are will be rendered through with holes that benefit an elite while abandoning the rest.

We can imagine that expansive military projects will capture his narcissistic imagination as expressions of his own inflated sense of self-worth. Impoverished areas of China will be transformed into segregated zones of exclusion and government control. The prison system will expand and mutate into a Gulag. Like Stalin and Hitler before him, transformed recidivist bureaucracies will become convenient dumping grounds for his more inveterate opponents.

President Jinping is not an aberration. He is the product of a Chinese political experience damaged by Imperialism and War, now dominated by the corrupting influence of money. Left unchecked he will be the first Chinese Fascist and this planet's first AI Autocrat.

In his own mind President Jinping sees himself as the answer. Ironically he will stifle creativity and funnel the energies of China into economic imperialism, colonialization, and war. Social media will be turned into an instrument of international warfare. Stolen technologies will be weaponized, and Communism will be transformed into Xiangshen. He will work to supplant the dollar as the primary currency of commerce and manipulate advantages in on shore productive capability to maneuver foreign policy. When the time is right he will entertain an idea of manipulating the US Bond Market with his $750 billion in Treasury holdings in order to de-stabilize the American currency and economy.

He will create a new Chinese digital currency. One with an implicit surveillance capability. The economy will devolve and require further oversight and control at the national level, a development that could evolve into a call for even more control and eventually the militarization of the entire Chinese economy. If the economy falters, war will be used to resuscitate the Nation. Conglomerates transformed into oligopolies will become the focus of government. The world will re-trench in response to this insular manifestation of Xi Jinping's Presidency. The scramble to control and federalize the remaining economies of the world and their associated resources will begin soon thereafter. Space with be militarized. Localized low grade conflicts will soon follow.

President Jinping will then turn to vilifying Judeo-Christian religions. He will inundate Africa with war making capability that will motivate further efforts to affect resource monopolization. Debt owed to China will be used to enact foreign policy manipulations. This will set in motion the day these regions explode in military conflict. Is President Jinping a harbinger of the apocalypse? It is not within the realm of impossibility. President Jinping's Presidency is poised to evolve at an inflection point for the entire planet. His stamp would be on everything that follows, a kind of President Jinping sledgehammer effect on the future of humanity that has the potential for tragedy written all over it.

The ominous implication is that a militarized China would be transformed into an immense weapons workshop – an Arsenal of Autocracy. Communism and militarized nationalism will overtly merge and take on an irresistible urgency of action, which will threaten civilizations and induce China to impose a revised conception of Chinese Communist Manifest Destiny upon the World.

If there is an opportunity for hope, it may rest in the propensity for the world to stimulate China's interest in opening itself to the immense possibilities offered by a welcoming integration into the World community. The average Chinese citizen is no longer inured to severe hardship. Sacrifice for Party is now nothing more than a platitude. The Chinese people are ready to express themselves internationally and will do so with an open heart if given the opportunity. The great economic democracies of the world can show them the way.

Opposition to President Jinping connected to a convincing certainty of purpose and strength of commitment will win the day. This can be interpreted as the reawakening of a culturally stagnant Chinese society to the maledictions of a far-right pseudo-Communist Party. Rehabilitation, reformation, and restoration. These ideas only need to accommodate and recognize that the Chinese cultural experience is diverse and robust and strengthened by a recognition of its inherent plurality.

America has and will continue to benefit from the restorative benefits of immigration. It renovates the nation economically, culturally, and now technologically. In many ways immigration has prevented the US from stagnating. Diversity is its great strength. This is why it is all the more desirable that the US welcome Chinese immigration. Change the Chinese the description of Zouxiam as the path that is needed to emigrate to America, to a welcoming of opportunity. Acknowledge the mistake of the Chinese Exclusion Act of 1882 and pass the Chinese Inclusion Act of 2025. <u>Brain Drain China</u>. This alone would diminish the potential for war and put the spotlight on President Jinping as a mistake of Communist

Party domestic policy. This diaspora would energize America and impassion the international community to enthusiastically embrace the benefits offered by Chinese global citizenship. It will also serve as an effective counterweight to the Chinese march to homogeneity.

It is understandable that as China has modernized, it has experienced a divergence between urban and rural, and working class and upper class. What the US can do is instead take advantage of this disparity by welcoming the dynamism and creative explosion of possibilities that has transformed what it means to be a Chinese citizen unchained to express themselves in the world. This will stabilize the phenomenon that is the Chinese cultural experience that will refresh the idea of what it means to be Chinese. Western Democracies can start now by recognizing China's isolation and yearning for expression as a path to redemption for the unappreciated Chinese citizen.

The case against President Xi Jinping must be prosecuted aggressively. He is an evolving Fascist and an aspiring Imperialist. His goal is historical retribution and at a minimum he must be stalemated internationally. Break the Communist Party free from its complacency. China can still become the wealth creation engine of the future. The alternative is a Chinese descent back into dogmatic darkness.

The World would enthusiastically welcome, absorb, and adopt a flowering of the Chinese cultural experience. The creative dynamism of the hard-working men and women who are the backbone of the Chinese economic miracle were once an important part of the 'Beijing Spring' initiated by Deng Xiaoping. They can be so again to the benefit of all of humanity.

China - look to the innocence and immense potential of your children and then forgive and make peace with the world.

English to Simplified Chinese (using Google Translate)

PREFACE - google translate

阴谋论是真理的黑洞。他们被研究了很多，但从未被理解。这本书将试图澄清非理性，这是所有政治制度的标志，但它在共产主义宣传理论中占据了特殊的突出地位，现在在中国被用来合理化回归孤立和社会控制。人类已知的最强大的武器是谎言。毕竟，人类的合理化能力是无止境的，当被骄傲和权力所释放时，可以用来以赎回过去的冤屈和恢复种族和文化要求所规定的国家明显的命运的名义，使不可言说的行为合法化。

我们在美国和欧洲看到了这一点，现在从中国自邓小平以来的三代最高领导人所经历的逐渐收缩中也看到了这一点。第三个不再是共产主义的。他已经变成了一个绝对主义者、威权主义者和独裁者，他利用民族主义民粹主义的词汇来加强对党和人民的控制。他在邓小平发起的门户开放政策中，夺走了中国和中国人民特有的历史自豪感，并通过一个傲慢的计划将其转向国内，该计划有可能复活毛大跃进的进步漫画。

为了夸大政治合法性而向内看的倾向并不是中国历史上的文化动机，而是源于民粹主义者领导的所有政治运动。这种影响在欧洲正在增长，现在已经在美国的下水道中转移，即美国多媒体和唐纳德·特朗普的政治瘤。这是一种懒惰的尝试，通过使用对民族主义的诉求来操纵民众。

在中国，这种后退 2 步以向前迈出 1 步的新倾向可以追溯到宣德皇帝于 1434 年颁布的"海进敕令"，该诏书禁止大多数海外贸易和互动，从根本上将中国与国际贸易和勘探隔离开来：这一政策的动机是担心海盗和管理与日本等邻国的经济压力。当然，这也是导致中国对历史影响减弱的转折点，最终在毛大跃进的种族灭绝和悲剧中爆发。正是几代人对智力能量和创新能力的浪费，使中国容易受到帝国主义罪行的攻击，并失去了抵抗日本法西斯侵略的能力。骄傲和复仇现在威胁到中国作为国际社会独立但互补的成员与世界进行富有成效的互动的意愿。

世界各国政府面临的挑战是理解，需要从跨国文化多样性和繁荣的分叉拉力的角度来理解中国，以及以致力于共和共和国的单一人民的名义呼吁废除自决权的呼吁所要求的对牺牲和服从的狭隘呼吁。

当使用埃里克·霍夫 （**Eric Hoffer**） 在《真正的信徒》中提供的狂热主义描述来看待这种牺牲时，我相信可以创建一个框架，不仅可以解释他们对近平主席的奇怪支持，还可以用作如何有效对抗和防止专制民粹主义和法西斯主义在共产主义中国酝酿的基础。

中华人民共和国不再是全球的贱民。中国的经济帝国主义可以被挫败，但不能通过在文化上孤立这个国家。与俄罗斯不同，俄罗斯将继续与乌克兰进行军事接触，而近平主席只会因为中国民众与世界其他地区重新接触而感到沮丧。普京在对外战争中浪费俄罗斯的财富将打破他的控制。中国人对参与全球文化体验的不可抗拒的渴望可以打破他的控制。共产主义无法在一个致力于开放和透明的世界的耀眼光芒下生存。

需要促使中国继续向世界开放，这样它，乃至整个世界，都可以从它所拥有的创新和重塑自身的内在强大力量中受益和繁荣。

近平主席正在重新定位这个国家，以重新获得他认为作为这个星球上卓越国家应有的地位，这将导致中国走上孤立的道路。特朗普在美国做同样的事情意味着这两个国家正走在一条不可避免的冲突道路上。

需要做的是了解中国政体的特点，并努力建设性地参与国家对工业和利润的创造能力。有了它，人民将改变党，党将重组，以支持与世界建立更加包容、开放和互补的关系。另一种选择是回归无知和孤立，随之而来的是暴力行动的倾向。我们与中国交往的方式将决定地球的命运。对于世界民主国家来说，选择和结果在我们自己手中。

PRELUDE - google translate

在台湾头城附近的近海，一架遥控潜水无人机从中国最新的 09IIIB 型核动力攻击潜艇上发射。光纤电缆被切断。该任务在淡水、巴里和方沙附近复制。卫星使用位于甘肃省酒泉卫星发射中心 （JSLC） 发射的多辆反卫星动能杀伤飞行器进行销毁，其中一些飞行器自 2023 年以来一直在轨道上运行。位于马来西亚 Jahor 的美国努沙再也数据中心遭受了一场神秘的恐怖袭击，导致整个设施离线。许多马来西亚人死亡或受伤。Starlink 在台湾的访问是通过与马斯克预先安排的协议被拒绝的，该协议基于对特斯拉的秘密渠道威胁。中国的兵力投射在台湾周围，让美国海军敢于做出回应。特朗普会犹豫。中国将利用他的不作为来启动对军事援助的封锁。

台湾将指派一艘基隆（基德）级驱逐舰，由 2 艘具有超视距能力的光华六（光华）级导弹舰提供支持，护送一艘商船到港口。中国最新的 055 型隐形驱逐舰将无线电发出停止警告，然后从其单管 H/PJ-38 130 毫米舰炮齐射，损坏但不会瘫痪记隆驱逐舰，该驱逐舰将以其 127 毫米 Mark 45 进行回应。随着对抗升级，中国习安轰-6远程轰炸机将向驱逐舰和商船发射4枚YJ-83反舰导弹。两者都将被沉没。对峙的光华六号（光华）级导弹舰将向中国 055 型驱逐舰发射多枚鱼叉。它会裂成两半，几分钟后就会沉没。一架台湾 F-15EX 鹰 II 将同时发射 2 枚 AIM-174B 远程空对空导弹，摧毁中国獾。到那时，中华民国的战争就开始了。

澎湖县岛距离台湾海岸仅 45 公里（28 英里），遭到 2 艘新服役的 076 型中国两栖攻击舰的袭击。YJ-63 空射和 DH-10 陆射亚音速巡航导弹蜂拥而至并摧毁 ROC 防空导弹系统。伴随着对台湾防御阵地的猛烈轰炸和 2 个伞兵旅的支援，该岛将于第二天沦陷。能够投降的士兵将被转移到大陆接受再教育。

近平主席将要求美国保持中立，但美国已经开始通过增加航母编队和重新部署的 B-1 和 B-2 来加强其海军力量。一架中国远程獾威胁并穿透这些航母群的扩大控制区之一，被海军 F-35C 击落。届时，近平主席将授权发布逆向工程的俄罗斯鲁宾设计局波塞冬自主水下核鱼雷。它将产生水下放射性海啸，使 USS Gerald R. Ford （CVN 78） 翻滚并倾覆，并使整个团队失去行动能力。甚至在引爆之前，2 艘弗吉尼亚级核快速攻击潜艇一直在跟踪跟踪尾随航母群

的新服役的 周 级核攻击潜艇，火线引导 Mark 45 ASTOR 在释放后的几分钟内摧毁了中国潜艇。所有 4 艘潜艇都将丢失。中国不会知道她的潜艇已经失踪了 2 周。

3 艘俄亥俄级弹道导弹潜艇和 10 艘额外的弗吉尼亚级核快速攻击潜艇被公开为已预先部署。北京将通过部署东风-27（DF-27）来威胁该地区（包括冲绳）的美军，这是他们最先进的反舰弹道导弹，它使用高超音速滑翔飞行器机动到目标。包括韩国、越南、马来西亚、印度尼西亚、日本和澳大利亚在内的美国盟友将开始在东海和南海部署。俄罗斯将从鄂霍次克和符拉迪沃斯托克出动，朝鲜将威胁进行有限的交战，而这些交战将被忽视。中华民国将开始部署 M142 HIMARS 以及游荡和远程无人机弹药，以对抗即将进行的两栖行动。战争将陷入僵局，但对台湾的封锁将继续。接下来会发生什么将取决于近平主席和特朗普总统。

FIRE STORM – google translate

1

国家主席近平正在设置绊线，将启动这一切。他的台湾海峡联合剑 2024B 海军机动涉及 90 艘舰艇，由 153 架飞机提供支持，这是 3 年来中国最具侵略性的演习。这些演习旨在练习和模拟封锁。这些计划是基于近平主席认为特朗普会默许而发起的。

五角大楼的评估假设中国要到 2035 年才能以目前的投资水平实现军事优势，但这是不正确的。近平主席的战略是使用"积极防御"姿态的地区优势之一，这种方法受到毛宣布的启发，即第一拳是为了避免下一个 100 拳。这个概念也是基于这样一种想法，即应该惩罚一个人来教下一个 100 个人。特朗普将成为近平主席的学生，近平主席将启动他的"战争是政治的延续"的研讨会，证明出其不意的主干是将速度与秘密融合在一起，他将在 2026 年中期选举后发起这一行动。

近平主席当然会注意美国新总统，一个他能够操纵的人。正如毛的著名宣言，"我们应该支持敌人反对的任何东西，反对敌人支持的任何东西"，这将使特朗普感到愤怒和困惑，因为他幼稚而愚蠢，并且基于深谋远虑的恶意做出决定。起初，特朗普会克制甚至畏缩以回应公开的军事行动，但因为他是一个软弱的人，所以他很危险，这最终会导致他以压倒性的力量做出回应。然后，近平主席会发现他的中国支票结果是一个美国伴侣，不是因为特朗普的先见之明，而是因为美国拥有压倒性的军事实力，并且仍然得到自由世界的支持，尽管领导她的男人缺乏经验。

无知和非理性的陈词滥调是美国新民粹主义的关键组成部分。国家主席近平也在利用误导来操纵中国公众。问问习近平的支持者为什么他们听从他。因为他们非常顺从，所以你得到的回复往往奇怪地不连贯。为什么要支持一个撒谎、操纵他们的不安全感、公然蔑视他们的智力的人。近平主席成功地激励了很大一部分中国公众，这意味着他对他们害怕被党抛弃的恐惧有洞察力。近平主席在共产党内崛起，反映出他操纵的天赋，而不是目的或政策。他现在使用专制民粹主义的策略将他的竞选活动武器化，这意味着我们必须问他这样做是否基于对人性的深刻愤世嫉俗的看法，以及他是否会利用一种权利感来瓦解中国通过重新定位以支持一个更具包容性和开放性的社会而取得的来之不易的进步。

近平主席的支持者渴望归属感，但认为他们被轻视。他们被嘲笑为无知和好奇，因为他们经常如此。没有说的是，许多人顺从是因为他们害怕。近平主席的支持者因孤立感而感到尴尬，他们觉得精英的成功标准使他们变得无能为力，并编造阴谋和阴谋作为他们生活命运的理由。他们觉得背叛和勾结一定是他们被忽视的原因，正是在这种环境下，金平主席表达了他们对事实的不安，否则这些事实会让他们相信他们有错。正是在这种不满的阴沟中，一个新的中国专制民粹主义者发现他可以茁壮成长。

权力积累并产生一种维护和保护自己的压倒望。当我们谈论习近平时，我们谈论的是对权力扩张的渴望，这种欲望可以追溯到所有受个人崇拜启发的政治运动的开始。社会分层和等级制度加剧的不平等并非没有道理。当允许它发展成仇恨时，对激进变革的呼吁就会滋生一种拆除排斥和特权结构的愿望。准共产主义宗教运动也可以成为仇恨的源泉，因为它们滋生了不宽容和对正统信仰的奉献。因此，共产主义作为宗教的替代品，使用亵渎神明的思想来灌输不宽容，民粹主义者经常机会主义地利用这种观念来建立支持。

共产党把自己当作替罪羊并不是出于煽动变革的愿望，而是出于保持承诺的需要。这是一种保持奉献的动机，然后将其转化为权力、金钱和控制。共产主义作为一种宗教是中国第一个大众营销者。**The Party** 是中国第一个 **Influencer**。我们只需要看看现在以军队为代表的准政治运动，它越来越看起来像一个盈利和权力扩张的企业，而不是支持中国自决的防御武器。

近平主席将中共变成了一场承诺繁荣的政治运动，但也许更重要的是，它为那些认为自己被忽视的人提供了归属感。这种运动提供了空洞的赦免，在这种安排中，买方获得了确定性，以换取他们的忠诚度和合规性。这些教徒容易受到操纵，民粹主义或共产主义绝对主义者经常利用这个机会。

尽管中国最近的经历是不受限制的个人机会之一，但精英原则也被用来证明财富积累和机会分层的合理性。这已经发展到中国的奥林匹亚财富和社会分层水平，社会流动性也可以显示正在下降。户口不仅成为控制无节制城市增长的工具，而且成为保持对呼吁包容的人口控制的工具。它已经从控制移民的工具演变成社会控制的工具，并迅速显现为抵御共产党合法性受到侵蚀的堡垒。如果不加以制约，它确实有能力瓦解政治局，但目前仍然是党控制不可或缺的工具。如果采用更具侵入性的监控机制进行有效操作，它有可能将共产党变成一个没有灵魂的企业集团。管理不善就埋下了共产党灭亡的种子，因为中国民众拒绝以政治顺从的名义放弃提高生活水平的要求，而政治顺从与文化和物质利益排斥相结合。

因为中国的精英政治，就像美国的情况一样，已经变得分层，而且在许多情况下是排他性的，所以很大一部分人口越来越怀疑机会是所有人都可以获得的不受限制的经济准则。这种影响在中国越来越大，随着更大比例的人口参与提高生活水平，不满情绪变得多方面。它的例子可以在媒体、社交网络和地下政治教育项目中找到。也许更重要的是，漏洞百出的社会安全网意味着个人要为他们的成功水平负责，这迫使不幸的人不安地得出结论，即一些人的安全是通过减少其他人的利益来获得的。

零和政治是建立在恐惧之上的。害怕自己会被抛在后面。当人们认为这是基于罪恶和缺乏公平时，这种恐惧就会变成仇恨。恐惧为民粹主义者打开了大门。仇恨为公民不服从打开了大门。

近平主席的计划正在加剧经济不稳定，从而产生巨大的个人不安全感，再加上缺乏全面的社会安全网，准宗教组织介入以填补缺口。他们被迫转入地下，扩大了他们的合法性范围，进一步破坏了共产党目前声称的授权。这产生了一种强烈的变革欲望，这种欲望既保守又反动。当受到威胁时，这种观点很快就会受到指责，并且无法进行反省，否则就需要对环境和动机进行诚实的评估。重点将集中在近平主席身上。

对共产主义目标合法性的建设性评估也需要对动机进行诚实的评估。对近平主席来说，就像对任何政治家一样，将责任归咎于外部原因，比质疑导致失败的决定要容易得多。这是抗拒分析的，可以被植根于可证实事实的半真半假的假内容所操纵，但这也消除了自我评价和个人责任的需要。共产党的问题在于，随着社会分层削弱机会，将充满挑战的时期归咎于外部原因变得越来越具有挑战性，而对于那些以中国经济奇迹为荣的人来说，这变得无法调和。

近平主席是试图从普遍的挫败感中体现社会工程的一个现代例子。到目前为止，这是有效的，但对徐近平来说，它还没有表现为一场群众运动。我们看到，他正在通过循环使用陈词滥调的方式和他复活中共对党的义务原则来寻找这一理由。目前，他无法灌输牺牲是由于他自己反常的自恋，这就是对他作为党的领导人任期构成最大威胁的原因。如果国家主席近平失败，党就会在他身边崩溃。想想一位近平主席，他拥有邓小平般的信念，相信中国的创新能力、努力工作和体现个人成功的能力。他将是不可阻挡的。

在精英政治中，如果我们看一下以共产党为导向的社会福利，我们会看到这些计划经常将人们冻结在原地，因为它们会导致不作为和自满。这是因为这些计划是折衷的措施，阻碍而不是促进这些人口有效地重新融入劳动力市场。中国活力的基础是个人可以重塑自我，但完全错过了最初使他们在那里的宏观经济压力。户口和自给自足的工资只会使问题长期存在。

显而易见的事实是，自由市场和共产主义经济原则之间存在的脱节往往跨越着无拘无束的劳动力市场的想法，而这种想法不能在中国持续存在。这演变成权力斗争，而这些斗争没有充分认识到经济再平衡造成的损害。当流动性在没有程序化的社会支持结构的情况下被阻止，或者被允许但被旨在冻结人口的官僚计划所阻碍时，那么从完全成本的角度来看，这种错位比专注于在经济投入和产出之间建立平衡的系统要昂贵得多。很快，事实也变得更加明显，它还孤立了工人，使他们与共产党分离，消除了共产主义提供的安全感，不再使人们相信中国新共产主义民粹主义的劝诱信息。通过这种方式，人们在努力在经济上重塑自己时，不会变得更加依赖，反而会更加独立。

中国正在重新演变成一个世袭制度，它在封闭的权力循环中运作，切断了不属于特权社会结构的人们获得机会的机会。结果是普遍的挫败感和不满，这显然是变革的预兆。这将需要国家主席近平寻找更多方法来加强支持。近平主席试图做到这一点的一种方式是排挤中国社会科学院　（**CASS**）　的分歧和批评，那里不再允许独立思考，员工被迫报告不服从党的路线的同事。这是学术界平庸的预兆，因为"拦路老虎"正在被"思想追随者"所取代，他们把研究建立在"高等理论"之上。通过这种方式，金平主席试图控制那些被剥夺权利的人的思想，他认为必须让这些人相信外部世界不再是好的。近平主席正在将失败外化，并表达这样一种观点，即曾经平衡和公平的东西已经被扭曲，有利于以美国为首的少数几个选定的国家。通过这种方式，他利用民粹主义来暗示艰难时期是捏造和故意设计的，目的是让少数人获得优于多数人的优势。

在中国，乐观主义现在是处方。中国人在资本主义中被教导"创造性破坏"的概念，但对于那些没有党员的人来说，这个过程显得冷漠、贪婪和阴谋。中国的安全网是以党为基础的，但这使得中国工人容易受到党对行动自由和机会和就业的控制限制。在美国，安全网很容易获得信贷，在欧洲，政府建立了全面的社会安全网，以促进社会稳定和促进重新融入社会，从而减轻经济流离失所的影响。在中国，经济和社会控制旨在最大限度地减少社会不满的可能性，这些不满会引爆挑战共产党控制的内乱。

在中国，就像在美国一样，那些逃离经济混乱的人在内心深处质疑自己能力的有效性，并担心自己主动避免经济衰退的倾向。对于那些能够保持地位和安全的人来说，目标的毅力和应得的回报的价值，都受到一种意识，即环境、地位和运气在他们的成功中发挥了作用。他们对自己地位不稳定的担忧促使他们延续党员身份所提供的现状。通过这种方式，对变革的渴望和保持社会或经济优势的需求来自同一个源头。当这种情况发生时，就为一种想法奠定了基础，这种想法操纵被剥夺权利的人和有权的人，其承诺信息与默许党的政策所提供的信息相同。

锦屏追随者并不渴望改变，而是渴望可预测性，并担心被排斥，因为他们无法获得稳定的生活质量机会。这促使他们采用否认自决的文化框架，并倡导他们认为能够提供安全的官僚机构永久存在。有趣的是，这种观点并不适用于那些认为自己的状况最绝望或最幸运的人。这些社会异类过于关注连续性，无论是从生存的角度，还是从维护权力和特权的角度来看。

相反，存在于社会上层和下层边缘的光谱感觉像是他们受到了不可预测性的冲击，当情况恶化时，他们只能自生自灭。他们意识到自己在社会中的地位受制于反复无常的经济状况，因此他们害怕改变，这让他们感到沮丧。当失业、健康状况不佳和社会地位容易受到削弱时，对保守主义的渴望就会占据上风。这既是维护社会地位的愿望，也是重新集中指责的动机。

幻想破灭的共产党人失去的不仅仅是他们对制度的信心。他们对共产党的合法性失去了信心。他们环顾四周，看到的只是混乱和无目的。他们的阴谋论观点是，恩惠和特权在一个不平衡的不公正领域被腐蚀。修复已经到来。他们觉得自己很孤独。难怪他们要么转向异见，要么对近平主席作为专制民粹主义者感到宽慰。

对于绝望的人，近平主席提供的口号被重新解释为一种信仰。通常，这个口号与千禧一代的成分有关，正是在这一点上，习近平将把他的支持基础变成一场群众运动。这些口号毫无意义并不重要。事实上，它们需要歧义。他们真正需要的是千禧一代的组成部分，包括为那些自认为是选民的信徒所承诺的稳定和繁荣时期。

然后，希望可以由仇恨孕育而来，在那里，承诺充满了谎言和缺乏实证证据。逻辑需要严谨。阴谋论只需要由拒绝相互矛盾的证据的意愿所支持的信念。锦平主席的信息是懒惰的、懒惰的、容易生气的，正因为如此，它很诱人。特朗普，实际上是每个民粹主义者也都在使用这种技巧。

共产主义意味着对当下的拒绝，这预示着特权的侵蚀。这意味着权力的持续减少，然后被定义为衰败的迹象。这意味着地位的丧失，一种植根于恐惧的零和视角。一种滋生仇恨、口号和千禧一代主义的恐惧。

这种对未来的处理方式要求对现在不可信。对事实的漫不经心的处理和理性的论证为民粹主义的阴谋论信息铺平了道路，然后被那些觉得自己被剥夺了繁荣机会的人鹦鹉学舌。它为道德妥协打开了大门，也为金钱、地位和特权的操纵打开了脆弱的大门。与金钱联姻的共产主义是肮脏的利润，它总是被那些提供它的人用来实现短期利益。它经常被用来推动除了少数人手中的利润和权力之外没有任何价值的思想和政策。这是对贪婪的轻松诉求，也被用作短期的合理化，但代表了对马克思列宁主义原则的不可逆转的妥协，给人一种党是寄生的印象。

中共中央政治局常委纠缠不清，迫使他们所有人为了生存而不断关注利润，这使他们走上了一条往往微妙但不可避免的腐败之路。难怪更广泛的中国公众越来越如此低估政治局。每个党员都应该得到它。他们听从资本主义奸商，而不是公民的利益。他们使用近平主席关于"治理中国"的四卷本谩骂中毫无意义的陈词滥调和政策论点来转移批评，这些谩骂对普通中国公民没有任何实质性的帮助。空洞的政党原则被用来掩盖所有其他问题。

正是在这种环境下，作为民粹主义者的近平主席（以及唐纳德·特朗普）发现他们现在可以蓬勃发展。正如美国需要的那样，需要剥离和禁止在担任公职期间的所有投资，这样影响力系统就不再凌驾于政策之上。剥夺非党员的选举权导致了不满。不满导致了异议。异议导致叛乱和对共产主义教条的拒绝。在共产党政治中，金钱是一种排斥政策。党是服务，或者说是利润。它不能两者兼而有之。

调查中国的任何一家商业企业，你都会发现近平主席的追随者正在施加影响。他的操纵力量无处不在，为忠诚带来繁荣。因此，普通中国公民经常会留下他们被不公平的当前环境所拒绝的印象。党的声望对这部分人来说没有立足之地，因为他们因为被拒绝而感到被贬低。

不要介意知识精英认为近平主席软弱且容易纵。使用农村局外人的语言，金平主席将自己描绘成他们的拥护者，并以这种方式动员了没有安全感的公民。实际上，他认为他们是消耗品，同时将自己置于他们之上，成为最值得拥有特权的精英。

近平主席的选民已经根据美国的成功标准来评估自己，发现自己不足。当将自己与民主精英进行比较时，他们发现自己总是排在第二位。即使是那些已经实现了一定程度的相对成功的细分市场，仍然觉得他们是在外面看。这些人正在寻找目标和认可。他们希望感觉到自己受到重视，而不是被遗忘。从某种角度来看，他们从什么原因获得归属感并不重要，重要的是他们属于哪里。共产主义是一个毫无意义的集体的例子，旨在创造那种社区的感觉。难怪近平主席不贬低毛。这样做会削弱他的支持者从中获得的包容感。实际上，这是一次秘密握手，可以立即成为锦平主席的集体成员。

共产主义陈词滥调的琐碎也为近平主席提供了机会，将他自己信息的毫无价值归入外国阴谋的非理性中。然后，金平主席的支持者将获得一个团体的成员资格，这对他们来说提供了一种归属感，而以前他们认为自己是难以忍受的无关紧要的。

近平主席的战略是通过重拾过去和重新塑造现在来重塑国际格局。事实上，这已经从他对台湾日益强硬的姿态开始，他对南沙群岛的事实上的吞并（这种吞并与乌克兰的经历有一些相似之处，但并没有得到足够的讨论）以及他在非洲的经济帝国主义计划。

对抗中国民众的无助感，需要的不仅仅是西方的创可贴政策声明。近平主席的支持者开始对自己以及他们作为中华人民共和国公民的地位失去信心。反驳近平主席的陈词滥调，需要肯定他们不仅作为中国公民，而且作为全球社会成员的地位。事实对被毫无意义的共产党陈词滥调打击的中国公民来说很重要。中国工人越来越意识到，他们的价值远远超出了他们作为劳动力资源投入的地位。单相思会滋生不安、激动、异议和叛逆。

具有讽刺意味的是，近平主席的党员也无可救药地傲慢。这是以自私的名义制造的盾牌，也是为愤怒辩护的。这种愤怒的核心是以恢复中国在世界舞台上的卓越理念为名对他们的同事进行暴力报复。

共产党员通过告诉别人如何处理他们的生活来赎回他们生活的无意义。获得机会是中国这一部分人所关心的，他们渴望的是再次确认他们受到重视，他们属于自己。近平主席用恐惧来操纵这种担忧。他缺乏的是关于他的提案将对未来产生的影响的同理心。对近平主席来说，自由就是无政府状态。他所破坏的是一种对无处不在的机会的信念，这种信念利用自我实现作为一种与平等相关的感觉。这就是解开中国创造力的束缚并将这个国家重新介绍给世界其他地区所需要的。

资本主义自由市场原则强加给中国文化经验的破坏球与这个人特别相关。面对产品、流程和材料通常严酷的重新配置，他们感到完全无助。向流离失所者伸出援手是共产主义的基石原则，而比较优势和自由市场原则的理念与没有安全感的工人无关。失去收入和养家糊口能力的工人会感到迷茫、被抛弃和心烦意乱。未付抵押贷款、不合标准的住房和无法获得有意义的就业机会的前景进一步加剧了这种深深的恐惧感。2024 年，中国的抗议活动激增，这是因为中国的安全网是基于特权的，它使中国消费者屈服于市场过度放纵的令人发狂的变幻莫测。

这就是为什么近平主席的填海造地信息将继续变得更加尖锐。事实上，他必须这样做。这意味着，在国际政治中重申诚信的时刻从未像现在这样重要。用共和党右翼的"实际"民粹主义和反民主政策来迁就总统，只会让习近平更加大胆，忽视中国公民。只有参与到关于中国身份和文化的讨论中，开放、自由和民主的国家才能被听到，而近平主席关于美丽新世界的承诺也开始失效。

INSIPID INTEGRITY - google translate
2

现代西方思想将共产主义与独裁、独裁与法西斯主义、法西斯主义与邪恶联系在一起。但共产主义实际上是专制控制主题的变体，因此它不是一个独特的政治结构，而是一个采用技术（宣传）的标志来促进控制和限制权利的政治结构。近平主席的政治纲领采用了法西斯主义和专制主义的元素，但并没有宣称自己是法西斯主义的。欧尔班和普京还采用了这些旨在欺骗和拉拢公众的系统性政治元素。从这个角度来看，近平主席既不是斯大林主义者也不是希特勒主义者，而只是一个独裁者，面向一种种族权利理想，提出中国的创建是为了替代美国的西方昭示命运理想。

专制的倾向源于人类倾向于相互社会支持和安全的结构。问题在于，专制是联邦化、民主化或碎片化的政治进程中固有的脆弱性所产生的结构。在这些过程被削弱的程度上，专制政治生根发芽，并最终杀死了它的宿主，即使它存在的多元化过程。

中国国家主席近平假设，各种力量正在努力利用中共的成功故事，并暗示全球权利的邪恶转移旨在通过以腐败世界观的名义夸大权力的过程，悄悄地剥夺中国的权利。他的追随者被这个信息所吸引，并不是因为它合理，而是因为它允许他们属于一个提供获得选举权的党特权的团体。因为中国的社会流动性正在下降，所以这一承诺具体涉及什么并不重要，重要的是它承诺了能够接触到一个自我复制的社会精英。

这个新运动还必须验证和消除其成员在文化上失败的感觉。这是通过愤怒的言辞传递的赦免，也反映在他们的挫败感上。事件的情感才是重要的，而不是信息的质量。近平主席的信息逻辑无关紧要。毫无疑问地接受论点不是问题，而是对信息语气的吸收。这是欺骗性的同理心，这是一种未被认识到的脆弱性，它为异见人士或外部社会影响提供了充足的机会，以揭露习近平的共同富裕宣言，因为它的谎言是真实的。

国家主席近平的群众运动的脆弱性隐藏在将他的支持者转变为民主事业的机会中。中国仍然面临外部操纵的风险，这是中共热切宣扬的一个信息。但这是习近平控制的政治局试图维持权力的声明。从习近平的品格和行动角度追究他的责任是解决方案的一部分，但这还不够。西方需要将此转化为神圣的反专制事业，揭示阴谋是锦屏。

近平主席可能在道德上妥协，但他的个人失败与他的支持者无关。相反，通过强调他的修正主义共产主义理想，或他对中国民族主义的极端观点，这将让人质疑对他来说已经非常不合理的诉求的合法性。仅仅说习近平将共产党的授权商业化是不够的，相反，还必须在一个滥用和行动的框架内描述他，并发展为个人妥协的讨论。这不仅需要被传达为缺乏道德，而且被传达为一种嘲讽，这是他扭曲的世界观中不可救药的一部分。一旦完成，近平主席的追随者将开始质疑他是否适合担任领导人。"金平主席领导下的一个国家"可以作为一个战斗口号，将注意力重新集中在他这个一心想欺骗的人身上。

国家主席近平的运动中也蕴含着内部异议的种子。每一次运动本身都包含着一个新的、更极端的事业的潜力，正因为如此，习近平将不得不变得越来越极端，这可能会分裂共产主义右翼。当这种情况发生时，近平主席将被迫用诱发暴力来补充他的信息。

以这种方式，所有福音派政治运动都容易受到极端主义的影响，这为他们提供了一个平台，他们可以从中想象以虚构的对手形式出现的暴力。当这具体化为一场承诺清除敌人的军事运动时，传播革命的超国家动机将由此产生，这是中国作为政治进程施加影响力的强硬演变中不可避免的下一步。这将是一场输出到中国境外的革命，并将预示着美帝国主义霸权的瓦解。民主将变得无能为力。

共产主义只是一个幌子。习近平的信息没有逻辑原则。目前，只有毫无意义的比喻的口号构成了他的大部分谩骂。他如此自我陶醉，以至于他没有兴趣消化任何与他的议程不直接相关的主题。这是他最大的弱点之一，因为近平主席还没有表现出过去伟大的劝诱者所特有的多方面品质。他的信息是民族主义的，但很狭隘。他一直专注于基于历史侮辱的中国复兴理念，而没有意识到他缺乏灵感会淡化中国对他的形象。他是一名技术专家，而近平主席目前提供的唯一信息是一个模糊不清的共产主义理想，而不是一个关于中国进步的客观纲领。这使他变得脆弱。近平主席无意分享他的权力，但他不是中国。这是每个专制民粹主义者的致命弱点。

当近平主席开始赞颂那些以他为领袖的追随者的英雄和烈士时，他将开始尝试将一个有凝聚力的革命信息外化，这个信息不仅会指责他的敌人腐败，而且还需要他们在内部进行反制。到那时，他将发展到一个对美国真正构成威胁的阶段。复仇的宣言将凝聚在一起，如果他发现自己很脆弱，他将提出更激进的建议，以拯救中国的名义起诉敌人和破坏对手的稳定，这些行动实际上是他试图维持对权力的控制。

为了阻止国家主席近平，必须发起一场新的对抗运动。美国的宗教权利提供了一个令人不快的例子。将宗教和政治混合可能是一种值得怀疑的策略，但中国对宗教的禁令需要被政治化。需要利用崇拜自由的道德要求来合法地促进互联网的解绑，今天可以容忍地将其描述为中国社会控制的直接外衣。将这些重要的讨论从共产党之外拉拢出来，也有助于揭示这个组织是一个腐败的金钱和阶级仇恨的政党，而不是平等和正义的政党。

普京与近平主席的交往需要过分强调。提供具体的例子，说明俄罗斯政府如何不值得钦佩，而是与人民为敌。中国的媒体拉拢需要被揭示为任人唯亲，它更注重金钱而不是信息。近平主席从毛那里得到的"共同富裕"的比喻，需要被揭示为专制共产主义的狗哨。

中国社会科学院 （**CASS**） 应该被描绘成一个腐蚀中国媒体的部委，甚至超越了马克思主义正统的戒律，而近平主席的控制是为了个人利益，而不是为了国家的利益。高翔需要被描绘成一个习的托迪，由于资本主义的操纵影响，他被描绘成共产党理想的叛徒。表明总统已经成为一个牟利扩张的寡头资本家，致力于建立一个由习近平本人主导的大洋洲、欧亚大陆和东亚的区域等级制度。

这些想法有点阴谋论，因此有些问题，但还有其他选择可以让金平主席制造的混乱不那么令人陶醉。提倡社会保障理念并在纲领上支持自力更生概念的计划，会立即使他的信息变得不那么有效。这就是政治局如此坚决反对解散户口的想法的原因。如果在中国没有了限制的机会，共产党员不再相信在中国的成功与党的忠诚度有关，而不是个人的创新、创造和自我实现的能力。这个国家的悲剧在于，它包含了中国人自我主义倒退的种子，使其重新回到了全球二等公民的地位。

随着中国青年失业率创下 **19%** 的新高，男女性别失衡超过 **16%** 进一步加剧了这一情况，这使得惊人的 **3000** 万年轻男性没有交女朋友或妻子的可能性。这是中国最大的未解决威胁，也有可能威胁到世界和平。不需要有创造力就能想象这会在单相思的年轻人身上产生多大的愤怒，这种挫败感会引发社会混乱，并最终爆发出一场蔓延到中国境外的疯狂爆炸。

2024 年，中国有 1200 万学生从大学毕业，但青年失业率仍然居高不下。中国的年轻人抱怨他们"生活在历史的垃圾时代"。与直觉相反，这种共产党制造的社会错位政策揭示了中国社会监视和控制计划中止的危险。这意味着需要更多的监控来防止怀孕时确定的性别偏好，并抵消沮丧的男性的犯罪行为，因为他们继续向一个将他们与女性隔离的社会发泄他们单相思的愤怒。需要记住的是，针对女性的暴力行为也会增加，这将需要增加警察人员配备，加强司法系统，改善心理健康服务，所有这些都是为了保护中国的女性。

揭露共产党在这项政策上的任何虚伪都会削弱近平主席。有数不胜数的例子可以用来说明中国的弱势群体是如何被共产主义政策滥用的。用阴谋的酊剂来描述这一点，金平主席对这个话题的自满就会烟消云散。对于性别偏好和女性胎儿堕胎这种普遍的文化憎恶的悲剧，侵入性最小、最简单的解决方案是什么？除了对预防犯罪、司法和心理健康服务的投资外，对教育和计划生育的公平和增加投资也使妇女能够控制自己的身体和生活经历。这样就不需要颠覆性的政府或邻里监视邻居来报告邻居系统。

最后，近平主席暗示开放是他最大的担忧之一，这并没有错。思想自由已经并将继续丰富国家，文化多样性很容易成为华人侨民的最大好处之一，但现在无拘无束的文化选择给他带来的问题多于解决的问题，因为他试图实施他的社会、经济和文化凝聚力计划。近平主席必须控制对党合法性的反对思想的获取。对他来说，不这样做是不可理解的。对信息自由流动施加越来越多的限制不会导致中国拒绝近平主席。它对他来说不包含直接的政策风险，但会播下导致他被免去党内最高领袖职务的种子。

几代人以来，中国公民因为党的残酷而被迫进入一种生存模式。尽管国家是单一政党结构，但这已经与党产生了一种原子主义的政治关系，这种关系必然促进了自力更生。这些自学的中国公民对金平主席的信息最不容易接受。这种情况开始改变仅表明之前的经济挑战正在结束，具有讽刺意味的是，这为近平提供了一个可利用的机会。

中国正处于新一轮繁荣的风口浪尖，但近平主席似乎在外交政策上进行了不妥协的投资。这是一个基于中共教条的计划，因此它是短视的、狭隘的，并且会让一个现在意识到欢迎接受中国文化经验进入国际社会所带来的潜力、利润和承诺的中国感到沮丧。

近平主席的谩骂带有明显的虚伪味道。这个男人真的相信他所说的吗？我们想知道他那些明显毫无意义的陈词滥调是否只是一个缺乏任何伦理或道德护栏的个人的咆哮，还是无拘无束的自私自利的产物。事实上，他自我陶醉的尖锐似乎确实具有极度自恋和对权力上瘾的特征。无论原因是什么，也许包含上述所有因素，人类的理性化能力在被马克思列宁主义故意限制的头脑中是无限的。正是他信息的教条基础孕育了他基础中最糟糕的元素。

他的言论有一个经过深思熟虑的动机，即中国必须采取"一国、一民、一意识形态、一党、一领袖"的政治观点，以巩固他对中美关系的看法。这种观点正在为中国准备一项旨在通过暴力行动取得结果的政策的非常现实的可能性，正如"我们现在面临的国家安全问题的复杂性和难度已显著增加。...我们必须坚持底线和最坏情况（观点），并准备好接受大风和汹涌海浪，甚至是危险的暴风雨的海洋的重大考验"。

近平主席有意识地、毫不妥协地重新夺回历史领土遗产，这是双管齐下的。它主张中国民族主义，同时将注意力从内部对奢华派对生活方式的破坏稳定的文化拒绝上转移开来。这是对他在 **2019** 年发表的声明的卑鄙拒绝，当时他说：《如果国家撤退到与世隔绝的岛屿，人类文明就会因为缺乏交流而消亡。他现在将这一真理置于整个中国的风险之中，因为他认为中国已经或即将实现与美国的军事和经济平等。有趣的是，这种裁员也包含了他自己解体的种子。事实上，它已经开始了。

外国投资开始缩减，现在每 5 个婚姻中就有 2 个以离婚告终，内部开始在公民混乱中看到裂缝，如煤矿中的"报复社会"金丝雀，城市骚乱如5起大规模袭击和53人被谋杀，以及小学生受伤，自9月以来的6周内发生。警车已经开始驻扎在学校和托儿所。想知道这些袭击是否是由失业的单身男性发起的，这将是一件有趣的事情，这种文化影响在美国也经历过。这是中国不满情绪的一种新的、出乎意料的表现，这种不满情绪将继续增长。如果不加以控制，将导致广泛而激进的反政府示威活动，并演变为暴力。

天安门事件的错误在于，中国现在知道，反对权威的示威活动不可能在没有受伤或死亡的风险的情况下进行。默认情况下，任何反对共产党的自发示威都会促使政府做出积极的回应，而政府将准备用暴力来反击抗议活动。这将使持不同政见者倾向于准备同样激进的反应，这是内战的前奏。原子化的个人侵略将巩固并演变成地方性的游击队，有时是有组织的攻击，随着政府以越来越高水平的暴力作为回应，这种攻击将继续螺旋式上升。到那时，国家主席近平的合法性将消失，将他赶下台的过程将开始。

近平主席的世界观无意识地带有偏见，是一个值得研究的话题。事实仍然是，习近平的世界观是赤裸裸的种族主义，并且容易产生刻板印象，以至于拒绝多样性披上了法西斯主义的外衣。通过这种方式，习近平以一种影响和激进他的整个平台的方式吸引了他的选民基础中最衰败的分子。他的批评者可能会公开嘲笑他无法更充分地考虑普通中国公民的需求，但事实上，他对中国仍然被视为二等世界公民的反常和愤怒凸显并验证了他不断恶化的挫败感。他将不可避免地通过对台湾的攻击来调和这种脱节。它会发生。如果特朗普表现出在与习近平的关系中应用现实政治的意愿，那将在特朗普离任之前发生。

特朗普就像班**门弄斧（T口门弄斧）**　在木匠大师面前炫耀他的技能。特朗普是一个无知而令人尴尬的新手，他将被近平主席带到木棚，他将取得短期的军事和外交成功，但代价是中国与世界其他地区进一步隔绝。这将实现结束台湾政权的目标，但有趣的是，这也可能导致习下台，以及第三次成功弹劾唐纳德·J·特朗普，特朗普的任期后继任者在迁就独裁者方面将不那么顺从共产主义的意图不是在全球范围内整合，而是要占据主导地位。我们将体验到的是在政治光谱的极端进行的全国性话语。妥协的共产主义影响者和学者将可以自由地传播仇外心理，这种仇外心理将在中国政治社会中最糟糕的群体中争夺被接受，包括阴谋家、政治奸商、种族主义者、机会主义者，是的，甚至包括外国国家媒体渗透者，他们将成为近平主席的目标，以煽动最邪恶的情绪，并向他的政治基础中最弱势的人灌输吸引力。反驳论点将变得无效，因为上诉是基于情感而不是事实。这将导致的不是尊重的辩论，而是强有力地阻止异见，进一步将近平主席与中国其他地区隔绝开来。

与近平主席的争论需要被配置为逻辑反驳，试图用事实来解析他的谎言，但这也用尖锐甚至夸张的反警告取代了反驳，这带来了自己的情感义务。如果做得正确，他的边缘篱笆支持者将被诱导转向基于邓小平对中国重新与世界接触的未来评估的新当务之急。当然，这里的危险在于所有观点都受到了损害，这为双方的怀疑打开了大门。

要救赎那些认为自己在中国不可救赎的未被救赎的人，需要近平主席配置一个信息，利用不受结构化分析影响的比喻和陈词滥调。这些声明需要为他们的接受者提供一种方式，让他们在一场抗拒反省的辩论中迷失自我。这就是为什么近平主席（和特朗普）的基础保持不变，也是为什么它看起来不拘一格，包括政治机构中的种族、虚无主义、孤立主义和种族主义部分。从某些角度来看，中国越来越直言不讳地表达其反日情绪，这最近表现在对日本侨民的攻击上。

日本不承认其从南京开始的历史罪行，这是不可理解的。当然，这也适用于美国，以及任何一个国家历史上的帝国主义，他们都仍然需要为他们的违背人类行为负责。套用巴尔扎克的话来说，巨大的财富总是从犯罪开始的。对美国来说，这不是通过一项罪行实现的，而是通过两项罪行实现的——奴隶制的耻辱和对平原印第安人的种族灭绝。

对英国来说，这是一样的，帝国主义在中国和印度，乃至全世界的耻辱。每个国家都有要做出的补偿。想想外交绥靖政策的影响，这些绥靖政策基于承认帝国主义的耻辱，从日本、英国和美国开始，承认种族主义的统治和对光荣的中国历史和文化身份的削弱。它的影响可以重新开始和解，并本身使中国重新向世界开放。整个世界都会松一口气。可悲的是，近平主席愿意扭曲这种挫败感，牺牲日益多样化的中国现代文化体验，以追求他在中国的报复目标。

DIALECTIC DISSOLUTION - google translate

3

普通中国公民知道他们缺乏发言权，但他们仍然拥有持不同政见的意愿。为中国公众提供匿名政治表达的小型交通工具有可能显著改善中国人与本国和世界其他地区关系的看法。这将在他们心中产生一种意识，即通过公认的途径实现提高生活水平，有可能扭转当前的命运。他们目前缺乏安全网，并且系统性地意识到他们的担忧没有被共产党视为优先事项，这为他们全面拒绝当前秩序提供了理由。

人民党成为混乱的代理人，被用作一种手段，向过去的开放政策灌输所谓的表态合同。因此，该党被认为以对正统的义务为借口，虚伪地将自己定位于权力的扩张，以此作为排他性的借口。它所呼吁的中国公民阶层已经认为自己没有党籍就无所事事。这就是为什么近平主席的比喻"中国人民是伟大的人民;他们勤奋勇敢，他们从不停下脚步追求进步"，这对那些在外面观察的人来说是一个空洞的承诺。

经济不确定性会带来焦虑和恐惧，进而使近平主席的批评者队伍不断壮大。低收入工薪阶层的经济现实与共产党社会发展五年计划所规定的宏观经济要务大相径庭，后者在重新平衡劳动力投入时，没有考虑到那些在经济上漂泊不定的人。这是数百万中国人沮丧和不满的现成催化剂。在这里，我们再次看到了共产主义制度的失败，它歪曲了资本主义原则，并使近平主席的队伍膨胀为民粹主义者。具有讽刺意味的是，继续这些错位符合民粹主义者的利益，即使就此提供空洞的解决方案，这就是为什么共产党让教育系统支离破碎的原因。以社会控制的名义对人民施加限制的名义让它有害，这符合他们的利益。这使疏远永久化，并以爱国主义的名义助长了公民不服从，然后金平主席可以将其外化以支持中国的爱国主义。

另一方面，那些无可救药、顽固的穷人则被孤立在经济周期的变迁之外。他们既没有从社会主义共产主义的潮起潮落中受益，也没有参与其中。相反，是失业者内化了损失并产生了不集中的愤怒。他们曾经有权享受邓小平的开放和机会计划所提供的好处，但现在却被抛弃和不被承认，而那些通过党员身份控制资本的人则重新调整方向，支持与经济建立更有利可图的关系

涓滴经济学是在美国发展起来的一种思想，只不过是一种特权的特许权，一种经济学的讽刺画，说我会给你一点，这对我来说意味着更多。近平主席曾说过，"一些大腹便便的外国人除了对我们指手画脚之外，别无他法。首先，中

国不输出革命;第二，它不会输出饥荒和贫困;第三，它不会惹你。那还有什么好说的呢？剩下的就是，正如普京建立了一个新的寡头贵族，正如美国以精英统治为借口，将 **.01%** 手中的财富积累合理化一样，近平主席也创造了一个新的中国贵族，一个共产党资产阶级，它只不过是公然试图维护特权和继续获得权力。

在所有三个国家，基础都已经膨胀并变得越来越沮丧。这三个国家最终都会崩溃，因为这会在拒绝阶级分层的过程中崩溃。事实上，美国已经开始在向特朗普的法西斯主义行动中做到这一点。不幸的是，这增加了中国发生冲突的危险，并相应地构成了对美国增加风险的反击。用来暂时阻止腐烂的将是外国战争纠葛，这些纠葛将一个国家与另一个国家间接地联系起来，但即使是这些分散注意力的做法也会削弱每个政权，并导致其政治结构失去合法性。我们在普京试图将俄罗斯人民的注意力从其政府的失败中转移开来，就看到了一个现成的例子。普京这样做为他自己的罢免埋下了种子。近平主席和特朗普总统将经历同样的事情。

资本主义在中国的经济战略中仍然发挥着作用，但必须承认，不受约束的自由市场虽然高效，但本质上是不人道的。认识到这一困境，而不谴责资源和资本配置要求的必要性，如果为处于危险中的工人提供一个中国承诺的替代方案，他们将重新发出声音。认可和支持将使他们愿意在系统内工作，而不是公开拒绝它以支持暂时但不可预测的变化。否则，中国的活力将被日益增长的挫败感所浪费，挫败感将寻找一个地方来指责和安抚对未兑现的生活质量改善承诺的愤怒。

想想那些被比较优势概念取代的中国工人，一个被特朗普征收的关税和莫名其妙的习近平强制隔离主义夺走工作的工人，更不用说通货紧缩的危险了。这个工人现在可能会以复兴的美国的名义再次被剥夺他的工作，这对他来说会让人觉得是反共的。

政治局允许共产主义教条对资本主义的含义进行精心挑选定义，这是习近平信息的最大弱点之一。相反，它应该承认资本主义是高效的，但缺乏爱心，自由市场原则需要"社会化"，人而不是利润需要放在第一位。有趣的是，美国也将从这个角度中受益。这个想法可以被认为是左翼共产主义和右翼资本主义之间妥协的中点。近平主席可能暗示了这一点，特朗普对此表示搪塞，但显然利润对他们俩来说都更重要，这需要以牺牲每个公民的利益为代价来重新分配资本。

虽然根据共产主义教条是不可接受的，但这个过程确实产生了增长，尽管大部分利益确实归于富人。经济稳定被废除，取而代之的是通过经济错位实现的效率。用资本主义的术语来说，就是对生产能力的"创造性破坏"。向国家讲述这个明显的事实已经被中国媒体噤声，这为现在由国家主席近平领导的共产党鹦鹉学舌的创造性谎言提供了力量。

对于普通工人来说，对失去某样东西的恐惧总是比对得到它的希望更强烈。一个明白自己的地位很脆弱的员工会给人一种并非错误的印象，即他的劣势为他人提供了好处。这个想法是，解决方案已经到来，输家是他。这成为一个无法容忍的想法，很快就会导致仇恨，而仇恨很容易滋生暴力。近平主席将针对这部分人口，不是针对尚未表达不满的一小部分公民，而是重新评估整个阶级群体对党的稳定构成威胁。他将利用他们的脆弱性来煽动民粹主义，旨在维持人民对共产党不现实的催眠信念。

近平主席的学说是流动的，但不受修改的影响。和特朗普一样，他的信息将焦点集中在他作为一个品牌的政策上，而正是在这一点上，他仍然很脆弱。近平主席的想法尚未围绕习近平是救世主的概念凝聚在一起，他的总统任期是命中注定的——他已经间接地提出了这一点。不过，这也有可能把他变成一个笑话，使他变得脆弱。在美国，正是因为这个原因，特朗普被认为是一个小丑。近平主席机械般的面容，他单调、干巴巴、反高潮的口才，表明他缺乏灵感和好奇心。近平主席沉闷而单调的虚荣。这是一个未利用的机会，希望回到邓小平与西方和解运动的批评者必须利用。

近平主席和他的追随者谈论党的忠诚度，但事实上，正是投降的这些方面导致了他的支持者感到焦虑。主动出击的自由将成功的负担放在了个人身上。当规划要求市场动态时，这种情况就被打破了。赢家通吃，所有竞争都发生在党内部，而不是市场动态中，随着竞争超越道德礼仪的严格要求，市场会伴随着地方性的腐败。

对于近平主席的追随者来说，自由是一种负担。他们很乐意为了地位和安全而放弃它。这种选择的放弃正是近平主席所渴望的。他利用它来夸大权力，追求个人的美化，在这个过程中，他无可挽回地破坏了开放的承诺，而这个承诺被用来创造今天的中国的经济奇迹。

中国工人现在看到的是一个牺牲他们的稳定性和安全的制度，而有利于一个在少数有权的人之间分配利益的过程。他们看到一个政治局准备倾听金钱利益，而不是公民。这就是为什么近平主席的支持者开始质疑共产主义的合法性。习近平没有改变共产党，而是吸收了共产党。希望重新获得影响力的邓小平政策战略家必须认识到人民的实际关切，同时将习近平塑造成一个对普通工人漠不关心的民粹主义者和骗子。

这就是为什么近平主席继续专注于忠诚，以击退内部和外部的反对者。主动权的自由被重塑为无产阶级的牺牲。通过这种方式，他消除了任何异议的机会。具有讽刺意味的是，正是这种对个人化行动的屈服，为他的追随者提供了摆脱自身缺点和失败的感觉。

近平主席的支持者渴望在这场运动中迷失方向。独自一人，他们是脆弱的，作为一个群体的一部分，他们不会因为在家里的行为和工作表现而被无情地评估和重新评估而令人沮丧的不安全感。他们渴望逃离无休止的战斗，比同龄人领先一步。

渐渐地，近平主席正在将他的信息从一种义务转变为一种学说，这种学说承诺一个拒绝古典共产主义的制度的成果，因为古典共产主义无法提供重组后的中国所能实现的好处。以这种方式，近平主席的支持者并不渴望行动自由，而是在习近平重新定义的利益和正义体系中实现平等。

近平主席的税收结构让整个中国都为他的虚荣项目买单，包括他的公路和铁路带项目。没关系，随着他将国家转向内部，这项投资的回报将变为负数。他的政党是其中的同谋，因为他们准备从这一努力中获得可观的利润。他们会繁荣昌盛。国家将受苦。政治局直接或间接地串通一气，推动资金使这种罪恶永久化。共产党，就像美国国会的情况一样，已经被金钱腐蚀了。除非对资本配置过程进行广泛的改革，透明地促进所有中国人的社会稳定和机会，否则就不可能进行有意义的改革和恢复对其制度的信心。

在金平主席的领导下，公民感到被孤立和受到体制的攻击。教育提供了一个特别尖锐的例子，富人有无穷无尽的途径来捕捉世代相传的机会。这与美国所经历的腐败的精英制度没有什么不同。哈佛因其"基于传统"的招生过程的虚伪而被斥为一个腐败的例子。这个过程已经表明自己被金钱、权力和权利感所俘虏。它充满了虐待，以至于它已成为贬低美国精英的最大原因。唐纳德·特朗普就是这个系统的产物。一个好奇心强的人，不读书，根据媒体的好感度来做决定。他是沃顿商学院的产物，沃顿商学院的录取过程通常将财富置于能力之上。美国和中国都遭受了这种扭曲的晋升过程。这些扭曲的人能够上升到显赫的地位，说明了美国和中国的教育体系已经支离破碎。

近平主席和特朗普总统是政治提炼过程的例子，在这个过程中，危险的前兆被允许留在政治汤中。他们最初可能会让选民陶醉，但最终他们会杀死主持人。

和特朗普一样，国家主席近平也是政治傲慢的一个例子。国家主席近平不断鼓吹对中国经济例外论的经济劝诫。这是有目的的误导，旨在将注意力从他的计划使最大的 **1%** 的共产党员受益这一事实上转移开。必须做的是通过提供中国过分的例子来突出这种伪装，就像俄罗斯前爱国者异见者在报道索契普京宫殿所做的那样。展示习近平的计划失败的地方，并强调对党财富的滥用，包括他们的飞机、他们的房子和其他奢侈品收购，这些收购使普通中国公民的困境长期存在，而不是解决。愤怒会越来越大，他的支持也会减弱。

中国的金钱使那些没有钱的人的声音无效。强调这一点，并展示近平主席、地方长官和中国企业集团如何利用金钱来操纵政治政策。揭露习近平和他的共产党的欺诈行为。公共服务不以营利为目的。难怪这个被遗忘的中国公民拒绝接受近平主席和他的共产党老卫兵。每个成员在某种程度上都是同谋。

在中国，信息的自由流动正受到攻击，可以预见到会有更多的限制。共产党的改革将停滞不前，除非实现透明度，并有机会对政策和官僚程序提供批判性反馈。必须提供外部信息来源，证明近平主席是局外人，并深深植根于这个侵权制度。揭露他是一个根深蒂固地腐败交换条件的政治进程的熟练操纵者，将大大有助于暴露他和特朗普一样的欺诈行为。

近平主席在中国的支持率是模棱两可的，这意味着中国普通公民对他的领导不冷不热。在侨民中，这一比例为 **35%**。鉴于目前党的参与率实际上只有 **7%** 左右，近平主席面临着动摇、失去国家对马克思列宁主义的冷漠。共产主义在苏联失败是有原因的。马克思主义是基于一种虚构的，这种虚构不断变化以适应当权者的需要。这是一个明显的谬论，只能通过编造宣传来确保。实现这一目标的最简单方法是继续对台湾采取咄咄逼人的姿态。这里的危险在于，这变成了一个自我实现的预言，与西方的军事冲突是不可避免的，从金平主席目前的说法来看，这似乎并非完全不可取。

但所有这些都错过了更大的图景。如果他成功了，那将预示着中国经济和文化奇迹的收缩，并意味着一个由人工智能支持的无处不在、无所不在的全国性监控社会的成功实施。这将预示着人类将迎来一个全新的危险时代，这个时代将在习近平的狂热民族主义纲领中诞生，而这个纲领是由中共专制政权巩固的。

针对 **93%** 不享受党员身份好处的中国人口。促使他们将自己的生活水平与更广泛、更开放的全球经济和文化框架进行比较。这将需要向个人揭示他们被党诋毁，这种脱节可以用生活水平的降低来代表。中国的贫困率是否大幅减少并不重要。在评估身份时，没有人会查看他们来自哪里。我们都只关注我们想去的地方，以获得我们所没有的东西。放大后，这种单相思会转化为公民不满，不满会转化为公民不服从，不服从会转化为内战。过去曾有人试图强调近平主席在这方面的虚伪。应该再做一次。展示他和他的主要贡献者继续将不满情绪外包出去，以积累金钱和权力。

对近平主席日益增长的怀疑将开始与中国无产阶级脱离关系。用社会主义提案作为补充，这将在中国农村和城市之间创造公平的竞争环境。这将提出支持结构，使提供给农村公民的利益相等。将重点放在中国工人的生产力和收入潜力的损失上。这将产生对就业不公平的认识，并且通过声明这些做法被用来限制工人以将机会引向他人，这将立即使锦平主席的提议变得不那么吸引人。如果做得好，它会在他的队伍中制造愤怒和分裂。

极右翼共产党人似乎无意中利用了一种双管齐下的方法来制造愤怒，以产生对政策的默许。他们一方面强调文化衰败，另一方面无情地攻击民主（美国）制度不公平。当人们考虑到从社会稳定的角度来看，中国的男性出生率仍然不可持续地高时，对文化习俗的评估并非没有道理。

当这也从失业的复杂问题，更具体地说是青年失业来考虑时，你就有了拒绝共产主义进程和政策的强大动力。法律与秩序被专制民粹主义者重新解释，暗示需要对政治进程进行更大的控制，以恢复文化和社会机构的稳定性。但是，当从中国以外的机会来看时，就会出现对不受共产党控制的信息的不可抗拒的渴望。

经济上的混乱也会破坏家庭纽带，这是中国文化生活的一个重要方面。尽管共产党强调家庭结构稳定的必要性，但共产主义的牺牲原则与这种对社区的奉献呼吁相矛盾。共产主义政策实际上加剧了这种脱节，这为民粹主义者提供了一个机会，可以传播产生狂热和仇恨的信息。仇恨不可避免地导致暴力。经济混乱是民粹主义和近平主席政策方针的必要前提，因为它为他提供了提出扩大社会控制范围的程序的理由。

突出国家经济机会和社会基础设施投资差距的比较，将激发对近平主席进步承诺的讨论。如果这在中国以一种易于理解和有意义的方式存在，那么近平主席永远不会发展到他目前享有的影响力。习近平从不谈论改善教育、失业补偿和公平医疗保健的具体和直接的建议是有原因的。它对他的分裂和操纵计划毫无成效。

中国的政治制度是说教，而不是教。西方来源必须教导，而不是说教，并提供促进自力更生的支持结构的例子，所有这些都在一个促进个人价值的包容性系统中进行。希望需要取代无助。目前，中国的社会安全网除了隔离接受者之外，什么也没做，从而为近平主席的"国际紧缩计划"提供了现成的订户。

近平主席的支持者们不顾一切地逃避他们参与中国政治进程的无意义。对他们来说，公民身份的负担已经转化为个人的牺牲。西方需要为他们提供在经济和文化上重新加入国际社会的机会。最终，我们所有人都将受益 - 中国人气的减少，以及中国外籍人士对习的批评的增加传播。为了对抗近平主席，需要表明他的目标是继续牺牲被遗忘的中国无产阶级，以便使新的中国共产主义资产阶级贵族受益，而他的纲领只是一种幻觉，旨在帮助他维持和扩大权力。

近平主席的学说不仅培养了对他的敌人的敌意，而且也培养了自己的队伍中的敌意，因为他的追随者们用奉承来争夺认可和认可。我们只需要看看共产党内部已经存在的争执和中国社会科学院 （**CASS**） 长期存在的宣传恶作剧就知道了。

我们看到的是，习近平的追随者是忧虑的、不信任的、怀疑的和空洞的。他们的目标缺乏定义，以这种方式，他们抓住了最不关心他们意见的人的赞誉和认可。这在他们心中创造了一种服从，但这种服从是在没有羞耻感的情况下被采纳的。这种划分显示了近平主席如何保持对共产党的控制。它旨在将支持重点放在总统身上，而不是原则上。它是浪费和脆弱的，因为这种内部控制资源的支出削弱了党。习近平触及的一切都是伪装。本着民主包容的精神和邓小平四个现代化纲领的复兴，从马克思列宁主义的束缚中解放出来的社会主义原则。然后，金平主席的欺骗和权力扩张学说将被揭示为只针对这个人本人，以威慑整个国家。

COMRADES and CAPITALISM -
google translate

4

如果你教孩子仇恨，他们最终会学会不尊重他们的老师。在大跃进期间，有 **30** 到 **5500** 万人死亡，其中大部分是由于当地共产党干部通过控制食品分配加剧了局势。这种政策与斯大林使用的政策令人不安地相似，这将导致乌克兰大饥荒的罪行和悲剧。在此期间，中国学术界的排名也将大幅下降。共产主义原则过去曾被用来为犯罪辩护，现在又被用来为犯罪辩护。

共产主义拥护国家进步的共同目标，但现在正试图用对资本主义的公共方法来覆盖这一点。这已经把共产主义变成了对原则的歪曲，甚至对资本主义戒律的抛弃。近平主席的纲领既不是共产主义的，也不是资本主义的。它所做的只是将 **Profit** 夸大在少数人手中。相反，必须做的是表明西方的资本主义方法通过优先考虑市场需求来更广泛地分配利益。这是必须传达的，以便为反对近平主席的紧缩计划建立堡垒。市场和银行改革、社会服务的公平性、支持性的工人赔偿和再培训并没有孤立工人，以及彻底改革的个人破产法、长期且资金充足的心理健康和成瘾康复计划，以及改革后的刑事司法系统，不起诉违反教义的异端。这是国家主席近平永远不会实施的，也是世界民主国家产生的信息反馈所需要的，以重新定位对中国政府的看法。

资本主义促进了投入的重新定位，当这种投入是劳动时，这会产生放大的不安全感，从而产生一波又一波的心理困扰。显然，这是一个适合煽动性的领域。近平主席的计划旨在放大这一制度的弱点。换句话说，利用自由市场的错位，让受影响的人倾向于拒绝它，同时嘲笑这个过程是反共的。这有多么不合理和矛盾并不重要，重要的是它为支持专制控制的错位发声。

它与旨在培养和支持自力更生的制度相反。习近平以巩固权力的名义这样做。就像户口一样，它造成了不平等，本质上是不稳定的。在评估经济利益时，必须考虑满负荷生产的总成本，包括与就业破坏和国内迁移相关的成本——包括身体、精神和政治成本。当这些成本从对犯罪和心理健康的影响方面得到全面解决时，近平主席将在客观地将人文主义观点应用于资本主义原则方面取得长足进步。

最后，中国需要成为一个重视教育而不是国防的国家。习近平将如何支付？他已经多次在生产率较低、犯罪率较高和医疗保健成本较高的情况下做到了这一点。考虑一下影响。门户开放的共产主义没有被否定，而是得到了加强。通过谦卑地认识到每个人都是有价值的，即使强调一个国家和一个民族，身体政治也变成了自豪感的源泉。通过这种方式，共和国被转变为一个有凝聚力的整体，不受专制共产主义民粹主义病害的影响。近平主席和未来的民粹主义共产主义伪装者将被揭露为软弱、毫无意义、无关紧要和无能为力。

另一个必须面对的薄弱领域是，中国的理念为那些足够开明的人提供自我实现的机会，以利用马克思列宁主义提供的可能性。互联网财富创造引擎，以及现在通过军事投资以及基础设施和能源生产投资带来的财富承诺，只会让许多中国人对中共经济奇迹的承诺感到困惑和孤立。当这与极端的财富积累相结合时，例如中国百万富翁投资了 600 万美元的管道胶带香蕉，这些香蕉作为资产阶级艺术的典范进行游行，这不可避免地产生了对近平主席政府的不信任，然后反映在不满上，导致脱离接触。

对于邓小平全球参与政策的支持者来说，共同目标不应该被宣传为共产党的关注点，而应该在政治团体的层面上。不是将个人归入国家当务之急的决定，而是作为一种工具，让个人可以感觉到自己是正在进行的中国创新传统的一部分。共产党虽然有凝聚力，但在理想情况下是不必要的，因为提高生活水平、社会安全网和改善的全民医疗保健将使中国企业能够在不依赖政府补贴的情况下进行重组。

中共已经表明自己容易受到内部虐待，并且是资源浪费的低效行为。我们所需要的是宜居的工资和全面的社会安全网，这有助于而不是阻碍就业灵活性。想想看，中国公司摆脱了坚持中国教条的成本，以及补贴生产配额和竞争受限市场的严重浪费。好处将远远超过负担。

中国需要明确的明确实施信息和教育开放获取的具体建议。在共产主义控制的媒体网络之外建立相同的提案将立即传达对这一事实的认可。确认需要增加对社交计划投资的调查可以配置为开源，而不与 **Party** 特权绑定。通过这种方式，每个人都可以从存在于公平竞争环境中的经济中受益。无论与党的关系如何，每个人都会以相同的程度参与——这是共产主义的基本原则。

员工和支持系统的任何安排都应该包括雇主并使雇主受益。没有什么能阻止对资本主义的程序化方法也为公司纳入支持结构和稳定的过渡替代方案。只是不是从共产党经济裁判的角度来看，他们操纵了游戏，因为他们这样做是有报酬的。生产能力不应与竞争隔绝，而应以能够在国内和国际上创造公平竞争环境的机制来支持，并为提高劳动效率成本的综合计划提供支持——这是中国最大的比较优势。

Tempered Capitalism 是一种将工人从使工人陷入困境的非个人经济制度的残酷中解放出来的方法。如果这是开明共产主义的词典，那就这样吧。脱离政治偏见的官僚机构，为了公正而组织起来，必须以一种重新优先考虑将其重新纳入经济框架的方式吸收经济瞬息万变。需要记住的是，财富积累在少数人手中，伴随着迅速的社会分层和非人化的社汇谷，这本身就是不稳定的。就好像这个结构的重量在其基础上变得无法支撑，并最终在民粹主义错误信息、仇外心理和军国主义的内爆中自行崩溃。近平主席的解决方案将成为中国和世界的祸根，并将遭到美国的积极反制。

今天，中国共产党的信息有目的地无视解构。它不是真理，并且是故意可变的。任何试图将其合理化的尝试都变成了徒劳的尝试，以揭露信息的无关性，因为该信息并不努力建立一个事实框架，而是邀请他们参与一个狂热的虚构社区——信徒们一旦变得无动于衷，除非提供一个新的意识形态社区，让他们可以在其中表达成员的兴高采烈。

近平主席对伪宗教共产主义的呼吁也是公然虚伪的。中国已经是名义上的共产主义了。今天，它采用了资本主义通过法定货币转化为专制主义的标志。伪宗教共产主义者忽视了一个如此明显腐败的人，因为他的吸引力不是他的道德，甚至不是他的劝人改教的信息，而是他的力量宣言和他可以克服不开明和无能的机构的宣言——唐纳德·特朗普也使用了这种竞选策略。这就是产生一个新的、新兴的政治化共产主义资产阶级的原因，它宣扬扭曲的列宁主义中国文化优越感和昭示命运的学说。历史上不妥协的宗教运动的例子比比皆是。美国极右翼基督教民族主义者也利用这一点来增加影响力和获得权力，在这一点上，他们与努力产生影响力的中国共产党人没有什么不同。更棒的是，锦平主席的信息强化了正统观念。这是愤世嫉俗但有利可图的——一种在太平洋两岸都奏效的愤世嫉俗。

现代中国共产党人在某种程度上已经变得孤立和轻蔑，这只会加强他们对更广泛的中国的孤立感。这也为他们对近平主席的信仰创造了催化剂。中国沿海政治是美国复制的地理人口统计学，将农村人口描述为无知且容易被误导。对党的忠诚，以及对家庭和祖先文化联系的奉献，似乎是无可挽回的矛盾，但对极右翼共产主义者来说，这些想法是相同的，因为需要对自我和国家的指挥和控制，以保护公民和党的神圣性。更开明、受过良好教育的中国精英对他们的轻蔑，使他们产生了一种不安的信念，即近平主席的纲领是他们实现一个尊重共产主义传统的道德中国的斗争中不可避免的必要条件。另一方面，对于习近平的追随者来说，他为他们提供了一个欢迎的融合，包括特权和机会、军国主义的自豪感和目标、国家和公司，所有这些都在一个极右翼的党和国家的巨石中。

增加近平主席构成的危险的是他作为群众运动民粹主义者和军队领导人的号召力。默认情况下，军队是紧凑的、有凝聚力的和分层的。光荣的理想通常以宗教意象的形式传达给士兵。士兵不需要效忠民粹主义者，他只需要被告知是这样。忠诚、友情和有目标的暴力行动是士兵任务中的主要内容。这位士兵很久以前就接受了失去自主权的事实，并接受了他所效忠的不仅仅是他自己。他属于他才重要。他所经历的兄弟情谊在辅以半宗教的民意正统观念时，会显著膨胀，更不用说救世主的合法性了。

对近平主席操纵的动机进行更有针对性的反思，需要缩小对环境的考虑范围。意想不到的异议继续渗透到中国各地，这给国家主席近平的政府带来了焦虑，但可能会让西方民主国家放心，他的政治吸引力正在减弱。这还为时过早。目前的异议预示着不满情绪正在增长，一些文化分歧，尤其是青年群体，特别是年轻男性的文化分歧，似乎正在走向无政府状态，但这些数字的棘手性会产生误导。青年作为他们人生阶段的一个条件，本质上是不安分的。如果习近平为他们提供实现独立的机会，他们将迅速转变自己。

实现这样一个状态的任务很复杂，因为它受到中国男女比例失衡的限制，这可能是近平主席造成社会混乱的最大潜在来源。这是一场迫在眉睫的社会地震，只能通过战争来纠正。也许是通过释放 **16%** 的中国男性没有女性来对抗 **8%** 的印度男性没有女性。除非这种解决方案有效，否则这可以通过增加社会控制来更现实地纠正。女性胎儿的堕胎也必须被严格禁止，同时禁止彩礼传统。国家主席近平面临的问题是，加速的社会控制计划将加剧异议，进一步孤立被剥夺权利的中国人。中国已经受够了。它的公民不想生活在"信息茧"中。这对 **Westen Media** 来说是一个机会，因为不平衡的复制动态强调了一个共产主义政策破坏了人类最基本本能的体系。只有过度的社会控制才能克服混乱，预示着一个政府对自己的政府发动战争的时代的开始，思想警察成为复活但现在无力放弃四旧——旧习俗、文化、习惯和思想的时代。这将是中国终结的开始。这将是共产党永远无法从中恢复过来的巨大倒退。

这意味着，美国提供的高等教育机会的欢迎承诺可能会使高考和公务员考试无效。这将证实，社汇谷华和户口是一个过程的制造部分，其目的不是为了强加公平和社会稳定，而是为了延续特权。这意味着，这将成为中国社会分层制度的永久组成部分，只有习近平政权的解体才能结束。

有趣的是，美国也在努力解决这样一种观点，即社会流动性已经通过限制公平获得教育机会而无效。在美国，它已经转变为对精英政治理念的歪曲，这种理念已经表现在向共和党右翼的政治举措中，这种政治举措包含了需要帝国总统来改变制度的理念。美国也在为教育投资不足付出代价。结果，一个特别没有好奇心、无知和不合格的总统，他会让国家难堪，让世界感到沮丧，并用他对东方的种族主义观点威胁中国。这两个国家都会发现他们正处于一个十字路口，因为改革将使他们走上公平和正义的道路，或者这种转变将促进权力的膨胀，特权和繁荣被分层，以保持对人口中其他更反动的部分的零和控制。中国将被束缚和贫困，美国将被剥夺她创造经济灵活性的能力。这方面有充分的历史先例。否则，每个国家都受益于中国的活力和美国拥抱多样性的意愿。全世界都会受益，但中国本身就是受益者。

这就是近平主席的中国民族主义纲领的大谬误。这是一个基于民族主义自豪感的谎言，实际上是为了巩固近平主席作为伟大领袖的理念。它最终贬低了整个中国人民。近平主席不是国家，他是国家的管家，而且是一个短视和危险的国家。什么时候一个人做所有决定是好的。从不。

中国的教育缺乏全球视野，它仍然是狭隘的、有偏见的和种族主义的。它刻板印象并否认历史，包括或可能特别包括俄罗斯和中国共产主义犯下的罪孽。刻板印象会阻碍理性思考。这是被禁止的历史。这是可怕和危险的。允许孩子被教导仇恨的父母会发现，最终他们的孩子也会学会忽视他们。

通过扩大中国公民使用西方教育网络的机会，并将其与贷款减免相结合，使习近平失去合法性。与此同时，一项扩大的贸易计划不仅局限于离岸，而且支持和保护西方制造业的卓越表现。这将使很大一部分中国年轻人摆脱他们对总统的优柔寡断，因为总统说他们应该 "吃苦"。这将导致他们寻找替代方案或要求改变习近平的治理体系。

170 万中国人被监禁，是世界上第二高的监狱人口，仅次于美国。近平主席注定要扩大这一群体，这将导致一个无视改革或为所有公民提供救济的政治制度。习近平宣称，苏联体制失败是因为它在意识形态上变得自满。他强调，必须将党用作社会服从的工具。然而，苏联并没有因为未能遵守正统教义而解体。它失败了，因为共产主义本质上是非理性的，需要一个监控社会来支持其政治结构的不合逻辑。中国需要的不是条件反射性地收紧控制，而是向中国公民社会开放，接受与世界进行富有成效的重新接触的承诺——一个愿意欢迎中国传统精华并将其吸收到他们自己的文化框架中的世界。这将是全球多样性的盛开，并预示着全球人类潜力的新时代的到来。

另一方面，中国人口结构的老年人福利正在逐渐减少，这很快就会达到一个拐点，人们意识到近平主席的排斥计划也是为了使他们处于不利地位。应该积极开展一场强调共产党政治局在这一领域的虚伪的媒体运动。将此与对当前规定性救济计划的批评结合起来，你将发起一场公关运动，表明中国老年人的独立性是以有利于成员身份的更高、定义模糊的共产党命令的名义而牺牲的。

晚年阶段的中国公民感到被社会轻视，必须证明他们毕生为中国做出的牺牲被低估了，并且被估价的水平不承认他们为中国目前的成功做出的贡献。提供部分救济的计划通常比完全没有计划更令人沮丧。他们对这个群体进行分层和细分。这个群体仍然具有可塑性，因为他们的脆弱性可以很快转化为一种意识，即他们已经被一个人控制的政府系统永久遗忘了。

另一方面，年轻选民的参与问题不是冷漠，而是不感兴趣。年轻人天生就躁动不安，因此容易受到影响。挑战在于为他们提供具体的例子，说明一个国家如何促进和培养他们向独立的过渡，使他们能够暴露存在于政府控制之外的机会。强调他们作为西方公民的参与需要责任感，但也包括承认当他们被允许探索职业选择作为自决原则时，他们可以有所作为。

异议能力不应被描述为一种缓和剂，而应从长期的角度重新构建，它承诺提供西方机构的近期支持，不仅针对批评的想法，而且提供解决方案和替代方案。近平主席的政府需要被描述为没有提供不同意的机会，因为中共拒绝这些想法对他们的社区和家庭有价值。党派对背离教条的批评等同于缺乏对个人的支持、尊重和关心。证明该党是由无耻的伪君子组成的，他们撒谎以获得支持。

那么，如何用对多样性和开放性的新热情来重新吸引中国年轻人呢？**K-Pop** 是一个可复制且不可抗拒的例子，但美国多元文化包容性的吸引力也提供了机会。旨在展示经典美国对创新理念的接受程度的媒体，但也对中国文化体验的美感感到惊奇，然后将中国视为互补的全球亲戚，这将证明缺乏阻碍习近平政权的洞察力。印度侨民被允许在美国创造奥林匹克级别的财富。为什么不去中国尚未开发的智囊团呢？谁会受益？每个人 都！除了一个例外，两个苦涩而孤立的老人认为，只有凭借他们神圣的领导权，他们的国家才会变得卓越。直截了当的现实是，美国是创造中国财富的催化剂，美国可以带走它，但两个国家都会被削弱。

强调个人对国家和民主包容进程的价值。强调共产主义计划如何使人民失去平衡。展示新父母和他们的父母将如何在一个旨在根据关系而不是机会分配福利的系统中努力为他们的孩子创造更美好的未来。这将是一个强有力的信息，将共产主义政策孤立为极度冷漠和不公平。

更应该引起关注的是极右翼的共产主义真正信徒，他们表现出顽固的非理性。让我们承认一下，许多近平主席的支持者有一个令人深感不安的特点，那就是他们被仇外心理所扭曲，或者只是缺乏道德韧性。两者都使他们倾向于接受仇恨和不满的信息。习近平为他们提供了一个借口和出口，让他们免除对自己的行为和信仰的责任。这些人渴望被接受，因此会毫不犹豫地向总统承诺，而不考虑影响。这部分公众也倾向于将暴力合理化，以此来进一步减轻他们对当前情况的责任。

共产党必须被孤立，并与其他国际治理的例子区分开来。这需要对习近平的行为和行动进行否定，这些行为和行动需要被传达为不可救药的。极端分子需要被描绘成他支持的基础，同时强调他们的行为是反常和可憎的。共产党支持掠夺性经济行为、在印太地区的军事侵略和无视人权的声明令人遗憾，但最令人遗憾的是乌克兰对普京的反共和反帝国主义支持。习近平如此透明地这样做，作为使他在台湾的计划合法化的前奏，这样做也加入了普京和特朗普的耻辱。这是所有三个男人的弱点表现为力量。

近平主席被描述为一个伪装的自恋者，他显然是自我陶醉和自私的。他怎么可能不像据称是 120 本书的作者那样，乏味地阐述了他的性格和中国共产主义意识形态的美德。可能正是从这个角度出发，他发展了他对社会的零和博弈。他描述了一个纵以为少数人谋取利益的国际体系，即一群阴谋者。没关系，这是他积极努力实现的政治结构。他指出，其他人操纵系统以使其受益，其不可避免的后果是他们拿走了其他人需要的东西。这为那些过度自我陶醉的人提供了一个机会，让他们迷失在习近平的大谎言中，即外部势力正在拉拢政府。

邓小平的主角们必须把这些想法标榜为意图制造恐惧。他们是一个懒惰和短视的人的声明。结果，近平主席的追随者会更响亮地劝人改教，但这并非不可取，因为它进一步强调了他们支持的人应该被质疑为不适合领导。美国和俄罗斯也必须这样做。

事实证明，少数族裔对近平主席来说是一个令人担忧的挑战。他通过侮辱、贬低、再教育和隔离来承认他们。这是一种披着种族主义外衣的呼吁，奇怪地为少数群体提供了一块认可的遮羞布，同时又认为他们不符合共产主义的承诺，因为他们是经济寄生虫。

随着少数族裔群体达到更高的生活水平，他们失去了带有偏见的孤立契约，并且越接近完全融合，他们就越感到沮丧。他们越接近实现包容性，就越能感受到社会排斥。这就是为什么维吾尔人、土家族、彝族、回族和满族越来越大声疾呼地要求完全包容，这对近平主席来说是一个危险且可能灾难性的情况。正是通过这种方式，中国的少数群体对社汇谷华的信息变得敏感。他们被迫重新考虑他们与共产主义的关系，而共产主义拒绝在他们居住的地方满足他们的文化和人口需求。工业化民主国家必须做的是突出繁荣、社区和支持的例子，否则这些例子会通过欢迎西方社区来提供给他们，并说明共产主义的虚伪阻止了同样的事情。

这不仅需要从概念上呈现，还需要通过具体的例子来说明美国民主党的大熔炉如何在尊重文化传统的同时提高生活质量。多样性是美国最大的优势，这就是为什么唐纳德·特朗普是美国最大的危险。有趣的是，这种危险正在国家主席近平身上复制。这两个人最终会以一种自我强化的策略相遇，以抵消彼此。结果将是战争。

如果不增加社会控制的成本，就无法管理户口。有管理的迁移会引起不满。分层失业，尤其是年轻人的失业，埋下了政治公民不服从的种子。代价将是中国的军事化，因为国家主席近平利用这一工具来镇压异见并实施社会控制。否则，他还有什么其他选择呢？不具有侵入性但同时也与其他支持计划相协调的官僚监督将有助于这些公民重新融入经济框架。贫困者需要得到补贴。仅仅提出这些变化是不够的。他们必须得到积极的支持，否则党的腐败行为所表现出的完全漠不关心，将很快压倒近平主席作为共产党领导人所遭受的任何批评。

西方必须提供的是承认这些担忧是有道理的，需要得到解决。这也意味着少数群体不能被一成不变地对待。任何对这一事实的承认都将大大削弱近平主席的合法性。第一个这样做的国家将获得他们的支持，而这将以牺牲近平主席作为一个被强行压缩成一个民族的国家的合法领导人为代价来实现。

白宫提议建立中国文化遗产博物馆。支持每一位成功的前爱国者，以及侨民在美国经历的获得认可的艰难道路。**Tank Man** 必须得到总统的认可和自由勋章。纪念天安门广场的死难者。归还未经许可从中国带走的文物。您能想象其影响吗？中国将化为一阵阵的感激之情（和人为制造的愤怒）。美国总统在赞扬中国对美国文化体验的贡献时所表现出的直觉，以及承认中国种族主义的历史耻辱，将使这一行动响彻整个历史。它将恢复国内外对美国理念的信心，更重要的是恢复对中国承诺的信心。它将表明，我们所有人都可以成为希望和希望的闪亮灯塔，并且整个世界都将从欢迎中国融入国际社会中受益。我们更有理由承认，金平主席和特朗普在错误的时间是错误的领导人，我们都需要为和平罢免这两个人而努力。

GOOD BIRD, BAD TREE - google translate

5

明智的领导者会聘请有能力的合作伙伴。那么，为什么锦平主席和特朗普总统似乎都选择了公然阿谀奉承的副手呢？这是因为罪犯在专制民粹主义者提供的吸引力中占有特殊的地位——尤其是一个可以声称与他们有亲属关系的人。沙文主义提供了腐败的救赎，当可以将责任归咎于社会结构和环境时，结果是两位总统的热心追随者。

美国人根据发型和口号进行投票。在中国，支持是基于胁迫和拉拢提供的。在美国，基于一个笑话或侮辱，比根据候选人的性格、经验或对职责的忠诚的质量，更容易放弃投票。在中国，支持是通过通过宣传力量所拥抱的个人崇拜赋予特权来收买的。当金钱仍然是政治的主要动力时，这种令人遗憾的状态会进一步腐败。那些将自己的成功更多地归因于交换条件而不是义务质量的共产党员，会吸引中国最糟糕的人来为公共服务。政党计划充满了未知和不可知的受益人。共产主义的倡议旨在暗示一件事，但实施另一件事。在许多情况下，我们无法辨别它们的真实意图。

无论如何，许多中国人要么没有意愿也没有兴趣去研究存在于他们社区之外的问题和动机。大多数人只是默许并希望最好。在最坏的情况下，他们的支持被放弃了，而没有考虑其影响。公民身份的无关性造成了一种无私的厌烦，给人的印象是，选民的意见被忽视，而有利于那些可以购买影响力的人。简单地说，为什么要不同意或争取变革。

在镇压天安门抗议活动时，共产党为普通公民埋设了一条让普通公民心怀怨恨、让不信任恶化的方法。为什么邓小平以屠杀镇压抗议活动是一个令人困惑和难以理解的政策错误，一个需要民族和解的骇人听闻的悲剧，而近平主席显然永远不会发起这种和解。这继续为不满的中国人提供脱离接触的借口。他们被灌输了这样一种想法，即在未来他们可能会成为改变的潜在烈士。

不幸的是，这也是在已经放弃思想自由的个人中产生目标统一的有效手段，通过合理化事件来巩固对一项被描述为比抗议担忧更伟大的事业的支持。这为近平主席提供了进一步巩固他对共产党控制的机会，共产党是一个分化、征服和巩固习权力的政党。

随着金平主席继续激进他的言论，他将这些行动呼吁发挥到了极致。他将自己推销为一位值得赞扬和忠诚的伟大领袖，如果需要的话，他可以作为一个必要的暴力变革推动者来追随。他这样做的威胁不再含糊不清。他监禁并暗示暴力威胁是对感知到的威胁的回应。事实上，他这样做是必要的，原因很简单，即围绕和平目标成立的组织是由基于对意图的个性化解释做出贡献的个人组成的。另一方面，发起行动号召并有可能施加武力的运动更紧凑，也更有凝聚力。它是一个团体所需的结构，它将个性融入到运动中。

这就是国家主席近平带领党前进的方向。创建一个基于定向行动的组织，试图重新发起毛主义起义运动——但这一次不可避免地通过外部暴力组织起来，以发起变革。而变革不仅意味着实现近平主席的帝国主席任期，而且意味着在政治进程的各个层面全面实施近平主席的政治机器，然后可以输出到国际上。这才是习近平提出的真正危险。这并不是说他继续担任总书记，而是他继续巩固对中国这个政治机器的控制。他将总统职位转变为新的毛泽东民粹主义独裁政权，使整个世界都处于危险之中。不幸的是，世界民主国家在短期内的唯一反应是在经济上进一步孤立中国，这使中国走上了与美国发生冲突的道路，因为它试图保持对任何剩余资源和市场的获取。

难道毫无疑问，一旦习近平巩固了对中国文化经验中各个层面的社会、经济和政治方面的控制，他就会把它们扭曲成将中国的霸权强加于世界其他地区呢？他对西方世界观腐败的指责成为他推翻整个国际体系的手段，以支持他将中国任命为全球苍穹中的卓越国家的愿望。

近平主席为中国制定的总体规划或战略路线图将包含与美国的短期妥协，但特朗普作为一个幼稚的政治无能自恋者，会将其误解为他有能力在国际舞台上谈判成功的例子。接下来发生的事情是，近平主席将利用此来放松美国的外交基础，然后对台湾采取低级的侵略行动。起初这些努力会被忽视，但到那时，这种暴力模式将使美国，即特朗普，接受他的意图，此时美国会表达愤怒，但从远处看，台湾实际上将重新吸收到中国的政治框架中将开始。特朗普虽然光荣而无能，但他将成为让这一切发生的催化剂。

如果以同样的方式回应，对台湾的全面攻击是不可能成功的，近平主席知道这一点。相反，暴力暗示的开始将凸显一种令人发指的无礼，这将有助于使他的观点合理化，即台湾必须不惜一切代价与大陆重新统一。这是每个民粹主义者都使用的一种策略，许多 20 世纪的例子可以用来强调这一事实。至于我们现在在乌克兰采取的 21 世纪例子，普京会失败吗？成功并不是他唯一的目标。与特朗普和 1

月 6 日对 **American Capital** 的攻击一样，目标是将愤怒和不满集中在此，这些愤怒和不满也被用作激进和暴力发起内部行动的借口，以平息不满和巩固政治权力。这些行动中的任何一个的危险在于，它们都会与内在的反叛倾向相抵触，这种不安太难以控制了。瓦格纳集团就是一个例子，中国也有这样一个集团在等待。

现代的变化是，终身民主党总统、帝国党主席和共产主义独裁者现在都可以通过人工生成的智能系统实现社区监督的"风桥"模式自动化，从而削弱自由，这将极大地扩大定向监控的能力。一个从 毛 时代复兴的计划，现在包括月经跟踪计划。习将通过大型语言模型，将监控能力的有效性从目前的**1500**万人的基准扩展到**14亿**中国人口，这些模型将揭示暗示异议的短语。不再需要筛选出对党派政策的潜在反对者。相反，人工智能确定的概率模型将计算异见概率，然后中国思想警察将使用这些数据来在有组织的运动联合之前将其消灭。中国将是第一个成功完成这一目标的国家。

在 2024 年的前 6 个月，中国司法系统以"散布谣言"罪起诉了 31,000 人。这个过程已经开始。世界民主国家注意到了这一点。您是下一个。

政府控制将在个人及其社区层面上释放出来。合规性将通过对社会计划、教育系统和就业机会的受控访问来实现。特朗普还将通过废除美国官僚机构的就业保障，用愿意以国家安全的名义颠覆美国隐私原则的忠实特朗普支持者取代"背信弃义"的专业人士来做到这一点。他这样做是为了降低这些组织的独立性，使自己离终身美国总统更近一步。

普京已经通过建立一个明显腐败和被俘虏的俄罗斯寡头政治来实现这一目标。国家主席近平正在通过他的党特权控制访问计划来做同样的事情。这三个人都将利用经济权力杠杆施加社会控制以巩固政治权力。他们似乎是竞争对手，而且在一段时间内会是，但最终会形成大洋洲、欧亚大陆和东亚的三重政治，这给人一种敌意的表象，但实际上却是为了引导对立作为社会控制的工具。

我们将经历的是，将地球划分为资源控制区，将繁荣等同于资源扩张的军事化。随之而来的将是控制太空的尝试，以及这个星球维持生活质量的能力的退化。到那时，骰子将被铸造。战争、社会分裂和人类未来潜力的丧失将表现为回归到适者生存的状态，这将预示着人类承诺的终结的开始。

这三个人都拥有一种顽固的自我合理化的精神病态能力。普京虽然在国内很强大，但缺乏在国际上施加影响的能力。他目前在乌克兰的努力将失败。特朗普虽然显然在情感上发育迟缓，在精神上受到怀疑，但有望被仍然强大的美国两院制所对抗。另一方面，近平主席不具备这些限制或限制。他是他的手艺大师，注定要做伟大的事情，虽然可怕，但很伟大。因此，中国的拐点成为世界的拐点。这就是如果允许金平主席终身不受约束地继续执政，他将构成的深刻危险。

终身总统确实很危险，它们不可避免地会导致暴力。虽然暴力行动有时不会成功，但它为民粹主义提供了好处，因为它的范围和侵略性不断扩大，并最终蔓延，最终影响整个国家及其军队。对于一位无拘无束的总统来说，这种情况仍然是一个深奥的危险，它可能导致公然强加一个基于资源垄断的新中国帝国主义，而这个帝国主义是由不可抗拒的中国军国主义支持的。面对对美国霸权的深刻威胁，特朗普和他的继任者们也将努力做到这一点。

对台湾的自发性和暴力性将使近平主席在世界其他国家面前失去合法性，但会巩固他作为人民的救世主中国领袖的地位。这将强化他们之间的观念，即美国必须受到打击，并将为继续采取深思熟虑的行动提供理由。一个由中国昭示命运的理念所决定的事业。没关系，近平主席蔑视中国人民。重要的是他们觉得自己属于一项伟大的事业，一项由中国新的专制民粹主义者命定的事业。

由此，近平主席将进一步尝试使当前的国际政治关系失去合法性。事实上，他需要这样做才能保持他的支持势头。没有这一点，他的运动就会瓦解，然后消散在孤立的疯狂阴谋论者群体中，这些阴谋论者会受到密切关注，但否则会被国际社会鄙视。然后，这些四分五裂的团体将再次转入地下，直到一个新的民粹主义者重新组织他们，并将他们是失败者的感觉转化为对美国的仇恨，他们的声音被释放出来，成为无知的骗子。

这样，仇恨就会成为近平主席谩骂的重要组成部分，这也是为什么他的支持者会欣然模仿他的风格。仇恨是国家主席近平的团结因素。他的追随者采用这种方法，因为它很容易。他们的懒惰说明了他们个人性格的腐败，就像他们支持的共产主义伪装者一样。这些辩证的毁灭门徒必须不断地被愤怒和嘲笑所刷新，使他们始终处于随时准备采取行动的状态。

国家主席的追随者放弃了保持独立的权利。对抗他们为他们提供了采取行动的借口，侵略的借口。这使他们更加不受其他选择考虑的影响。这是习近平不断强化的自我放弃过程的强化。他所谓的自发的震惊和敬畏行为，实际上是为了让他的支持者倾向于拒绝个人化的行动。它揭示了他们内心对"战斗试炼"的准备。近平主席在他的支持者中制造了一种感觉，即他们是恢复中国理想的不可或缺的一部分，因此党员们坚持不偏离正统的有条不紊的对话，或者假装是教条主义的马克思主义者。

更不祥的是 CCP 建立的社区网格管理监控计划，其中整个社区被划分为每个监控段 15 到 20 个家庭，并要求居民报告他们的邻居。这些"网格工人"进行了一种孩子气的展示，除了确认他们是懦夫之外，没有任何意义或实质，通过这种忠诚的表达表明他们可以纵。请放心，唐纳德·特朗普会对这种社会控制方法感兴趣。美国的新闻报道已经警告说，他有能力通过获得手机通话来颠覆隐私规则。这个邻居监控邻居的"网格系统"已经准备好通过 AI 实现自动化，例如 Co-Pilot Agents，它创建虚拟报告社区，其中关系被预先定位以生成监视警报。这种未来会激增 Co-Pilot Monitoring Agents，它们自动化一个"3 度分离"监控社会，通过浮出异议来确保政治合规性，从个人层面开始，立即与他们虚拟建立的电子社区重叠。

然后，**Crime Prevention** 与 **Social Control** 合并。思想自由变成了一种强加，通过电子户口表格进行监控和监视。这就是习近平的未来愿景 – 一个将提供给世界其他地区的中国昭示命运版本。这是一个明显而现实的危险，它将削弱整个地球人类体验的活力。没有哪个国家会比中国本身遭受更大的痛苦——中国是人为制造的文化同质化和平庸的新发源地。近平主席将用对技术实力的一致性感到自豪，取代他国家文化多样性的壮丽。它的中心将是中国宏伟的多元文化历史遗产的漂白。

如果不是那么危险，邻居报道邻居的可悲本质可以被忽略。在美国，**Nextdoor** 网站也展示了这种社区文明去进化的倾向，抱怨、谣言、人格破坏和对邻居的恶劣报告已经包含了该网站支持、合作和共享社区资源的初衷。所有这些都凸显了美国和中国社交媒体上人性最恶劣的常规化，这一过程由美国发起，但将在中国实现。

近平主席和特朗普总统已经利用这些通讯工具灌输了一种极端的服从，以至于如果它退化为暴力，他们都会借口这是反对者制造的罪行造成的，但他们自己却要启动这种罪行。从这个角度来看，近平主席不仅对中国，而且对世界其他地区来说都是一个紧迫的危险，因为其他民粹主义领导人都在模仿他的社交技术，从特朗普开始。通过这种方式，习近平将实现他的目标，即成为一个卓越的中国，成为世界其他地区的决定者。

近平主席所开辟的，是其他独裁者可以效仿的道路。这是在世界领导层面对近平主席的崇拜的开始。这些人将成为腐败的独裁者领导俱乐部的一部分，该俱乐部在全球范围内带来有害后果，因为他们都试图为他们的自恋和权力欲望赋予意义。

民粹主义领导人所做的是努力煽动（或利用）国内不稳定来获得支持。必须通过加强两院制或议会结构来阐明他们的动机，以孤立他们对法西斯主义和煽动性的倾向，从打破产生专制政治框架的混乱的司法框架开始，来对抗这些人。隐私原则必须得到尊重。必须取消整合介质。

多媒体需要通过禁止自动链接推荐来受到法律约束。举个例子在美国，美国纳粹仍然可以链接到其他白人民族主义者，但他们必须手动这样做。否则，自动生成的多媒体推荐将成为虚拟"邻里网格"社会控制电子监控系统的基础。他们还将继续自我强化人性中最糟糕的倾向。如果在美国被阻止，这将随着中国进一步进入多媒体同质化而孤立中国。从 **Tik-Tok** 开始，没有什么比阻止中国基于人工智能的文化操纵的传播更有效了，因为中国发现自己在一个拒绝法西斯主义并欢迎开放和多样性的世界中越来越矛盾。中国将再次发现自己被孤立，对于新开明的中国全球公民来说，这是一个站不住脚的情况。

金平主席和特朗普总统的学说已经成为政治上失职者的堡垒，是无意识和无知者的贫民窟。它不受批评的影响，理性对其追随者毫无意义。习近平的追随者所感受到的力量不是来自他自己的内心，而是来自一种感觉，即他是比自己更强大的事物的一部分。任何坚忍的人所拥有的与生俱来的力量都是无效的。承诺源于一种沮丧，这种沮丧将自身定位为一种愿望，即打破那些会挫败他们经济安全目标的反对者的意愿。这是对拒绝自决的验证。近平主席成为上帝的替代品，他的政党取代了教会。接下来是对存在于这个承诺之外的一切的拒绝。中国成为至高无上。孤立主义倾向是这种影响不可避免的必然结果。它不考虑什么对中国有利，而是考虑如何巩固近平主席的权力。

孤立的普通中国公民感觉无能为力，但作为共产党的一部分，他们被动员起来，切实支持无懈可击的正统观念。近平主席所做的是为党员提供声称承认其价值的参与性替代方案。否则，他们会感到更加孤立和被辱骂。遵守要求的强大动力。唯一直接的对付办法就是把他们的共产主义傀儡变成荒谬的，对毛的模仿，甚至不幸的是到了阴谋的地步。近平主席要被塑造成一个小丑，一个红色的小丑，有着可笑的、石板脸的面孔，这是对力量的模仿。把他所有可悲的虚荣心描绘成一个被任命的领袖，他将被揭示为有害的，值得嘲笑和嘲笑。这是一种令人讨厌的策略，但它会奏效。

以爱国者游行来对抗近平主席，他们赞扬邓小平尊重中国的聪明才智和包容性的传统。赞美能够在文化上振兴中国的侨民。证明中国伟大的国家实验之所以成功，是因为这个国家通过邓小平（就像苏联通过赫鲁晓夫所做的那样）拒绝了煽动者，并且可以再次这样做。事实上，虽然近平主席试图表现出与过去相关的使命，而是积极地将他与现在被感激地拒绝的过去历史悲剧联系起来，例如大跃进的国家悲剧，同时也承认邓小平最大的错误是天安门广场大屠杀，近平主席从未谴责过这一事件。

证明习近平践行裙带之耻，欢迎金钱腐败。揭示他在优生学中暗示了有效性，并且他没有谴责毛泽东主义腐败的耻辱或天安门的耻辱。可耻的是，他的狗哨声说外国势力"如果试图欺负或影响国家，就会被砸脑袋"。这就是习近平的不谦虚。一个互补的中国在国际上将带来比军国主义姿态更广泛的好处。大声宣告。

近平主席模仿毛，这是一种耻辱。特朗普钦佩安德鲁·杰克逊（Andrew Jackson），他是美帝国主义的支持者，奴隶制的支持者，也是印第安人种族灭绝的推动者——这也是一种耻辱。

他们历史观的不合逻辑意味着他们的声明没有任何事实依据，只是他们在支持者中产生了一种印象，即他们不再被一个被描述为在利益分配中长期存在不公平的制度所忽视和遗忘。在某种程度上，这实际上是基于利润和权力的根深蒂固，以及对贫困者的剥夺，而中美的低层经济阶层则被要求在面对错位时实现自我。事实上，共产党将支持中国农村的计划定性为以繁荣换取安全的计划，可以而且应该被描绘成金钱利益的伪装，这些利益集团屈尊以牺牲他们本应服务的选民为代价来维持权力。

金平主席的幻想是一种滑稽的情节剧姿态，制造轻视并将其转化为犯罪。夸张的戏剧性对民粹主义运动并不陌生。他们变得越是可怕的极端，信息就越成为运动。

无论像"两个建立"和"两个坚持"这样无关紧要的口号多么不相关，其信息就越有吸引力。信息越炫耀，它就越能有效地获得观众。这就是为什么近平主席抨击不遵守共产主义正统观念的原因，以及为什么在每一次总统声明之后都必须利用他的垃圾言论来构建对立观点。在西方，他的言论被认为缺乏相关性而被驳斥，但这不是他的意图。近平主席的声明不是为了告知，而是为了诱导人们遵守。将他的信息与前爱国者一起漂白，这些人代表了中国广阔的海外意识，形成了一种独特而对立的视角。

金平主席平淡无奇，因为他需要如此。他是一个解构的民粹主义者。他之所以不引人注目，是因为没有其他可立足的地方。创造一种奇观将营造一种英勇的氛围。相反，他暗示他正在为身体政治牺牲自己，而实际上他正在用他的专制民粹主义毛泽东垃圾的涂鸦来玷污中国的政治制度。它是透明的，但很有效。另一方面，如果他把自己表现成一个愿意在体制内工作的诚实的人，他将立即失去对中共的控制，因为他将不再有任何可以提供给他的支持者的东西。他提供的机会是让自己迷失在一个旨在免除他们自决权的借口计划中。

新中國人对此的感受最为强烈，他们经历了一些微不足道的成功感，但意识到他们正在被一个超然的特权精英阴谋所虐待。在这种看法中，他们并非完全没有道理，正是以这种方式，共产党的特权对近平主席不利。对于近平的追随者，甚至许多有抱负的共产党员来说，党成为问题，而不是解决方案。

习近平在领导层上扮演角色，但他还没有用新的标志来充实自己的表演。直到中国领导的共产国际重新出现，这个共产国际被打上了国际共产主义的新标志，他才会从民粹主义完全转变为以共产主义为基础的专制法西斯主义。

中国仍然容易受到权力和仇恨象征的影响。言论自由仍然是一种特权，而不是一种权利，作为人性的一个普遍方面，中国也不能幸免于种族主义，如左翼、小日本、杨桂子、邦子和太八子等人物所表现出来。美国也遭受着这种无知的尴尬，正如在夏洛茨维尔的反犹太 **Tiki Torch** 集会上所看到的那样，可耻的是，一位美国总统也是一名被判犯有性侵犯罪的重罪犯，他认为自己不重要。欺骗是每个民粹主义者的纲领性，国家主席近平也不例外。随着仪式成为金平主席欺骗计划中越来越重要的一部分，人们将看到结构化的崇拜示威，这些示威会演变成仇恨示威。

近平主席通过编造一个神话来强化这一点，即中国共产党为回应腐败的西方霸权而采取了强势行动。他允许通过使用自我牺牲的意象来描述这一点。这些伪造是令人信服的，因为它们创造了没有事实的信仰。用假三段论合理化。

这是近平主席暴露狂耻辱的一部分，现在他的支持者们纷纷效仿。

假装是他计划的必要部分。它是无懈可击的，因为它与逻辑相悖。必须提供给中国的是一个借口，可以剥去习近平作为中共战士的面纱。他必须被揭示出他是一个软弱和腐败的人。这是他与特朗普的共同特征。

赞美他的卑鄙人物、罪犯、空洞的人以及那些引起厌恶的人也必须受到贬低。这包括他从圣洁的官员那里得到的谄媚支持。为他不那么顽固的支持者提供一个出口。这将放松他对公众的控制，否则公众会喘不过气来等待他的下一次侮辱和谎言。

揭开掩盖金平主席弱点的伪装。在中国公众面前游行那些被他的行为伤害的人。他的反应会变得更加尖锐和不理性，这会削弱他。加剧了他的自恋。保持兴奋。侮辱他。他生活在一个充满谎言和空洞赞誉的泡沫中。利用他的自恋来对付他，从而瓦解他角色的外表。这是他最大的弱点。否认他的自负和有限视角的合法性。让它变得尴尬。它会在他里面产生一种疯狂，使国家感到沮丧。

SLOW COOKED FROGS - google translate

6

近平主席必须赞扬目前的政府结构。他将其从建设性的东西扭曲成千禧年的技术乌托邦辩证幻觉，从而为他提供了一个平台，他用这些借口来驳斥对他任期总统任期的任何批评。他对中国许多罪恶的封闭观点直接归因于他的领导能力。这就是为什么中国的侨民需要将他个人的政治、社会和经济失败有纪律地、常规化地公之于众。他们还必须代表近平主席选民的人口抱负。根据他的失败对他人生活的影响来做这件事。破产、解雇、种族清洗、彩礼、女性胎儿堕胎。由于他的性格，所有这些都需要被传达为政策的失败。

他的虚伪不仅必须通过他所倡导的事业来传达，而且必须从他人格的碎片化性质来传达。他支持一个凶残的北科尔政权。他与犯罪的俄罗斯寡头结盟。仅仅说他撒谎是不够的。他给别人造成的伤害是真实的，需要被宣传。只有这样，他才会表现出一种令人憎恶的冷漠性格。近平主席的人格不洁。他对对手的憎恶必须重新集中于对他品格的驳斥。

近平主席故意将美国的经历描绘成一种痛苦，因为他必须这样做。这是有预谋的，因为否则他的节目会很无趣。从某种程度上说，他是一个不太可能的艺人，虽然他的信息经常微妙地注入了怨恨、仇恨和愤怒，但这正是他的支持者认为他是一位神圣的领导人的原因。他是他们的总统，是他们个人挫败感的代表化身。

他对外国人的嘲笑进一步强调了他的支持者所感受到的孤立感，以及他们从中获得的归属感。结束近平支持者所感受到的无助需要成为外交关系运动的一个有效部分。如果能有效地完成工作，而近平主席不回馈，将启动这一过程。习近平的"正面我赢，反面你输"的信条，在他的文化诉求中随处可见。以所经历的伤害来传达，重要的是他的伪共产主义辩证资本主义学说，将大大有助于放松他对原本被迷惑的观众的控制。

突出他角色的尴尬品质，但也嘲笑他最极端的支持者。他们并不构成他的大多数基础，必须被描述为他的教义的可笑例子。对他的支持者的极端行为的蔑视将开始转化为对这个人的蔑视，一个完全没有原始思想、行为和行为的人。

近平主席对未来的宣言既不可行，也不可行，只能提供将权力扩大到一个人的选择。西方需要提供更具体的例子来说明作为特权精英成员的近平主席与经济弱势群体之间存在的权力差距。展示他如何滥用破产法并伤害他在经济上限制的人。展示他所青睐的精英是如何单独受益的。请举例说明他愿意牺牲他人来换取自己的个人利益。创建一个出口，以重定向对向世界张开怀抱的中国的支持。

另一方面，煽动者总是希望重新集中责任，并规定通往辉煌未来的道路必须伴随着对当下阴谋犯罪的摧毁。言下之意是，腐败者不会在没有暴力的情况下放弃权力。然后，煽动者可以将仇恨引导为侵略性，这是控制不满者的必要必然结果。它不仅仅是一种令人上瘾的目标和自我牺牲的混合体。它是对其追随者沮丧的药膏。具有讽刺意味的是，这种仇恨的分享被转化为希望，成为救赎无价值之物的药膏。目标与承诺相结合，以减轻那些认为自己缺乏政治价值的人的不安全感。

革命的推动者发展了一个关于过去的神话，它与千禧年的未来理想相联系。通过这种方式，他们的追随者可以背弃现在。它是对过去荣耀的捏造，被用来拒绝此时此地。当这些过去的想法与未来的救赎联系起来时，概念的连续性就建立了，这需要摧毁现在。这样，现在就被剥夺了它的真实性，使它不受争论和妥协恳求的影响。这些运动的成员将自己视为神圣的战士，充满了口号和旗帜，传达了他们是被选中支持伟大事业的选民的信念。当这演变成自我牺牲，并被写进愿意被监禁甚至为这项事业而死的词典中时，该运动就准备扩大为有组织的暴力，作为实现目标的必要先决条件。

群众运动的组成部分将目光投向了当下的脆弱领域。不平衡和罪恶被用作剥夺合法性的理由，并暗示整个结构已经腐烂，需要拆除。腐败的司法或经济制度的含义被用来传达这样一种观念，即整个制度正在被陪审团操纵以培养异议。然后，个人有义务为支持人民共和国而进行激进的改革。这种地方政府的合法化成为形成由民粹主义推动的群众运动的门户。理性的变革支持者被描述为缺乏洞察力和对马克思列宁主义精神的承诺，这进一步迫使幻想破灭的人寻求保证荣耀的承诺。

传统上，共产主义劝诱者意味着可以通过执行共产主义教条或过去的正统原则来改善现在。这也是近平主席能够主宰党的另一个原因。他拒绝现在并将其合法化，声称当前的状况正在被外部自由主义动力无可挽回地破坏。在这种状况下，保守派主张对现状进行革新。

近平主席的目标也是要断绝对邓小平宽容中国形象的忠诚，并将其重塑成一个专制的摹本，献给一个以他自己为中心的强大领导人。这就是为什么对共产主义牺牲原则在哪里可以找到的怀疑与习近平无关。一切都被颠倒过来了。**Left** 是 **Right**，**Right** 是 **Left**。共产主义就是资本主义。当允许交互时，这两种方法都不会被描绘成具有合法性。只有近平主席的政党被描述为拥有解决方案，而且确实有义务带领国家走向未来。通过这种方式，习近平将马克思和恩格斯的原则归结为支持他成为下一任命运领袖的义务。随着中共继续妥协更传统的共产主义原则，近平主席将进一步巩固权力，而整个中国也将发现这些原则也都向他投降了。

自由派和保守派可以用近平主席的人性观点进一步推断出来。近平主席任性且以自我为中心，因为他在自己身上看到了这一点，所以他也认为这是每个人性格中难以解决的方面。其他人不能被信任或依赖，因为他自己除了对自己之外没有其他忠诚。这就是习近平走不信任之路的原因，也是邓小平强调可行的原因。邓小平认为，人的精神是软弱的，但可以通过强有力的纪律来恢复它。对近平主席来说，信任是毁灭的预兆。

有一个解决方案，尽管很危险，但特朗普很快就会如此粗鲁地意识到这一点。当两位领导人踏入对方言论的污水池时，他们会发现，起初双方都会在和解中扮演角色，但最终特朗普会通过他的代理人激起近平主席的不妥协。越是顽固不化的金平主席，特朗普的声明就越不理性，最终他和金平主席将被激怒到毫无意义的愚蠢，从而使他们俩都受到嘲笑。当这种情况发生时，近平主席会发现特朗普是最脆弱的，而近平会煽动这种不妥协，直到特朗普在他自己的愤怒下崩溃。

愚蠢就是愚蠢，特朗普将试图利用金平主席的主张来对付他。他将在 **MAGA** 淫秽的背景下这样做，并尝试将 **CCP** 描绘成新的邪恶轴心，而不是奉承的声明。特朗普将把这与阴谋论和共产主义吞噬全球的贪婪结合起来。近平主席的支持者会大喊大叫，但近平主席会无视这种暴行的肇事者。特朗普的虚荣心将是他的**毁灭**。与此同时，国家主席近平将慢慢重新定位中国，以对抗世界。

近平主席需要被描绘成一个畸形者，是对共产主义理想的粗暴模仿。在某种程度上，他鹦鹉学舌地提出了为正统信仰而牺牲的想法，从而玷污了他自己作为开明的共产主义变革斗士的形象。无情地甚至鲁莽地将他描绘成中国政治界的病。当国家主席近平他所能吸收的极限时，他将倾向于使用暴力，因为他认为周围的光芒被玷污了。如果他在内部诉诸暴力，无论是直接的还是通过暗示的，他都将失去人民的支持。把每一个极端的动作都附在他身上。强调他对过去中共制造的悲剧的无视。这将使他陷入矛盾的漩涡。他不妥协的本性将是他的毁灭。

目前，金平主席的选区更倾向于顺从的反动而不是激进。他们以自己在别人身上制造的嫉妒为乐。他们的不满变得可以预见，旨在让那些他们认为自己需要与之竞争的人感到不安。近平主席的《中国治理》为这一职能提供了形式，这也是他如此专注于合规的另一个原因。这不是支持的标志，而是表明他的家属从他们有效地责备非民选者并将自己置于优越地位的感觉中获得满足的程度。如果这些听众的注意力开始减弱，这将表明他的支持者不再从过去的国家不满必须得到纠正的想法中获得满足感。他的复仇计划将变得迂腐，并暴露他的原则是空洞和毫无价值的——一个民粹主义者为了逃避自己的不安全感而进行的阴谋。

这就是为什么近平主席必须继续劝说不切实际的事情。它为他的言论的无耻辩护，没有这一点，他在国际上制造的混乱就会使自己成为可验证的放弃的对象。对他来说，荒谬本身就是目的，当涉及到他用来支持他毫无意义的策略的策略时。最终，中国将失去与世界重新联系的恢复力量和多样性的恢复活力。整个国家将被削弱。

FRIENDS FROM FAR AWAY PLACES - google translate

7

近平主席认为，中国的经验本身就是目的。他这样做是因为这是他可以用来美化自己的骄傲的东西。他相信中国可以自我实现，并准备为这项事业牺牲他人，这项事业旨在获得权力、积累财富、获得赞誉并缓解对中国在世界上地位的根深蒂固的不安全感。这体现在他愿意考虑暴力行为以实现其政策目标。国家主席近平利用了他的支持者的希望和梦想，这些支持者也希望他们能够实现这种中国式的伟大概念。让国家主席近平误导公众的原因是他错误地意识到自己的傲慢是无法妥协的。一个更有操作天赋的经济管理专家会把他们的注意力集中在旨在维持和增加收入或平衡资源投入的系统和流程以及管理方法上。

另一方面，失败的管理者往往认为他们非常有资格在公共服务中取得成功。需要重新确认他们作为领导者的价值成为这种奇怪状况背后的驱动力，在这种状况下，失败的经理或党员变成了政治家。你不必在政治局的队伍中走得太远，就能发现那些利用政治作为平台来修复受损自我价值感的失败者。他们的无能成为他们在公共舞台上取得成功的动力。他们不顾一切地这样做，导致他们在领导道德上妥协。他们变得模棱两可，将其合理化为实现支持他们为国家服务的更大目标所必需的。他们唯一真正的目标是将权力和影响力转化为收入。

这就是为什么许多政客昂首阔步，对自己的成就表现出过度的自豪感，同时宣布自己是中国共产主义事业的仆人。他们的成功让他们觉得自己非常有资格领导。从这个角度来看，近平主席成为终身制并不奇怪，党员们准备牺牲他们的原则和品格来支持一个显然不关心他们的观点和动机，只关心它们如何为他的利益服务的人也就不足为奇了。

共产党员的动机是自私自利。他们的冲动在于否认他们认为自己是悲惨当下的一部分，而这个当下使他们作为自我决定的个体无效。这更加有效，因为他们缺乏对自我的具体定义。必须暗示的是，维护伟大的中国共产主义实验本身就是一个失败的事业。一个对整个世界和全人类都有影响的决议。

必须将锦平主席描绘成大骗子。在他的追随者心目中，把他等同于一个邪恶的伪装者。最糟糕的欺诈行为，因为它利用了他们的信任和灵性。国家主席近平利用他的职位来加强支持。用它来对付他，在他的追随者眼中制造恐惧和不信任。

习近平学说的荒谬谩骂往往显得如此公然的操纵和自私自利，以至于难以理解怎么会有人相信或被从他嘴里涌出的毫无意义的陈词滥调所吸引。但事实上，这些谩骂对于锦平信仰教义来说是必要的。这并没有在他的支持者中产生对他的真实性的怀疑，而是使他的论点不受真理的影响。他的声明是极端的，因此是绝对的。这造成了一种顽固性，保护金平免受相反论点的影响。然后，他经常断然拒绝任何可能与他自己对环境的解释相冲突的考虑。

否认这些声明就是质疑这个人本人的真实性，对近平主席来说，在一个信仰体系中，这是绝对不允许的，否则这个信仰体系就会在自身矛盾的重压下立即崩溃。

令人不安的是，习近平会在多大程度上拒绝反驳。他以这种方式行事似乎高深莫测且不合理，但这是近平主席掌权的严峻现实。在否认常识的同时，他也否定了他自己的个人感觉，即他的信息缺乏价值。

共产党员渴望不协调，把帽子挂在轻浮的胡言乱语上。他们的目标不是理解，而是暂停怀疑。这也是为什么金平主席没有解释他的目标，也没有提供政策细节的原因。创造理解会削弱他信息的力量。理解政策会使其变得纲领化和平庸，这就是为什么任何澄清或揭示他的承诺的空洞本质的尝试都无法吸引他的支持者。他的烟雾和镜子程序不能被直接攻击，因为它缺乏连贯性，因此不受分析的影响。

必须做的是攻击这个人自己。让他成为伪装者。打电话来质疑他对自己作为中国救世主的看法。剥去他的人格，揭示他无疑是那个满脸皱纹、无能为力的人。放松他对党的控制。他的支持者将自己与他联系在一起，以提升他们对自己的形象。如果锦平主席被揭露出令人厌恶的样子，他口是心非的性格会让他的支持者对他感到厌恶。这将导致拒绝将他作为榜样的人格作为被模仿的榜样。

近平主席的信息的合法性和信念不是必须被追究的责任，而是将近平主席作为中国所能提供的最好榜样的自信。相反，他必须被指责为中国人短视地关注贪婪和对财富积累的执着的最糟糕的例子。他应该被憎恶。只有这样，他才能成为被嘲笑的对象。如果这种情况开始在关于金平主席作为最高领导人的讨论中站稳脚跟，他将失去其职位的合法性。

近平主席的追随者们，就像近平主席本人一样，都是空洞的，因为他们在智力上很懒惰。这就是为什么近平主席没有兴趣或不愿意参与理性的争论或辩论。他需要保持不可理解的状态，以保持他的信息的顽固性。否则，他既没有时间也没有意愿开始进行学术活动。无论如何，这项投资的回报都不值得他投入时间，只会让他的支持者感到困惑。

这种狭隘的信息营销方法也是他最大的弱点之一。强迫他回答有关他对中国的文化目标、共产主义学术的目的、他对经济学的对抗性方法、他对道德小组的压制等问题。他作为人民之人的自我描绘是他的跟腱治愈。他在试图反击时会变得生动和难以理解。西方必须无视近平主席的做法，而是作为一个准备欢迎中国加入互补国际社会的国际联盟，继续展示经验和理性的能力。这样一来，习近平不仅可以被证明不合适，而且心胸狭隘，自恋地专注于他认为对中国最好的事情。

共产党学术界的不合逻辑缺乏洞察力，但更重要的是是一个谎言。通过剥离这种相关性的错觉来制造怀疑。共产主义是建立在辩证神话之上的，因此，党员很容易受到马克思列宁主义的嘲讽。从这些人的漫画开始，这些人是不是中国人意味着什么的奇特例子。创造这些神话制造者的形象，作为对近平主席的模仿，这将使基层共产党员感到沮丧，并引导他们重新考虑他们对一项不再为他们提供无懈可击的成本和收益分析的事业的承诺。支持骗子，你看起来像个傻瓜。更重要的是，你自己也成为了被嘲笑的对象。对于任何习近平的支持者来说，这都是一个站不住脚的立场。

近平主席的信徒们深感不安。不费吹灰之力就能引起对总统的厌恶。就叫它是什么，角色暗杀。这需要的不是他编造的谎言，而是为了吸引党员，他们会认为他们受到了锦平的不公平对待和故意忽视。如果他们认识到习近平将他们视为可以利用和丢弃的工具，他们就会远离他。事实上，有很多例子表明他已经这样做了。突出显示此项。近平主席是一个噱头。他的副手都是笑话。将金平主席的弟子与这个可笑可悲的人联系起来。然后呼吁他们作为一个伟大国家的公民，他们被欺骗和忽视，但不再被遗忘。

近平主席对中国构成的威胁部分在于他发起的运动的内在特征。突然的变化需要一个群众运动，作为一个有凝聚力的整体来回应。近平主席所要求的不容置疑的服从也要求他的追随者有一个可变的目标，一个可以被总统随意改变的目标。这使他有很多机会将他的运动转向暴力，如果它符合他的目的。事实上，如果他的支持开始减弱和破裂，他将无法阻止它。随着他开始失去对支持者承诺的控制，他的言辞将更加激烈。

中国越接近与美国的对抗，中国就会变得更加孤立。全世界都将团结起来反对近平主席。普京将提供试探性支持，但他无能为力，因此毫无意义。如果近平主席持开放态度，明智的举动将是恢复和扩大由邓小平开始并由江泽民加强的与西方接触的政策。让中国在国际舞台上蓬勃发展，中国将以其无穷无尽的能量和重塑自我的能力拥抱世界。否则，近平主席将发现自己有可能失去自邓小平以来中国所取得的一切成就。正因为如此，他将无法克制自己诉诸暴力。这是专制效力的巨大谬误，也是近平主席特别不适合担任公职的原因之一。

然后，美国将需要扩大盟友并与地方政府协调，以防止近平主席诉诸武力。为什么这很关键？因为当国家主席近平发现自己无法控制他在国际上制造的愤怒时，他会声称假旗行动。这将造成混乱，并进一步诱使极端分子在军事上对抗美国。如果允许这种混乱蔓延，将使习近平能够将西方定性为弱者。从这个角度来看，金平主席不会因为催化挫折而失去任何东西。唯一的解决办法是在法律和经济上孤立他，最好是在近平主席赖以产生储备货币的封闭市场范围内。美国需要向公众保证，美国仍然准备与中国重新接触，替代市场仍然安全，同时强调近平主席正在国际上煽动不稳定。焦点需要继续狭隘地指向习近平，因为他是一个已经失去了对自己和党的控制的人。

近平主席对中国与世界其他国家的地位产生的疏离感，是他用来为军国主义奠定基础的东西。对目标的极度热情只有通过释放行动才能实现平衡。暴力威胁是习近平用来让他的外国对手失去平衡的手段。他将美国描绘成无能的，如果他的追随者爆发对美国的谴责，那只能说明美国不公平地维护其作为世界最大经济体的地位是有错的。这将成为特朗普需要应对的矛盾而困难的困境，无论是作为潜在的中国对手还是贸易伙伴。国际上必须从法律角度做更多的工作，公开强调对中国极端分子的监控正在进行中，军国主义是不能容忍的。

近平主席关于国际秩序操纵的声明需要在对整个国际体系的易于理解的评估中失去合法性，因为对近平主席持续诋毁美国的努力的有力驳斥必须常规化。在不受审查限制的中国征求公众意见。这将使气泡收缩。证明国际体系的碎片化性质也使其不易受到操纵。强调中共试图限制讨论的尝试花费了大量的精力来捍卫站不住脚的东西。让他们去吧。近平主席越是大声谴责这一过程，他就越接近被人怀疑。

最后，积极揭示近平主席的经济影响力来源。共产党在这里仍然很脆弱，因此需要用恳求和改革建议来反击。将财政支持与中国的收入分层联系起来。将腐败与不断增加的暴力事件联系起来。将此与受影响地区得到近平主席支持的共产党代表联系起来。必须注意将重点放在那些与总统有直接联系的人身上。利用这一点来强调共产党的虚伪，以此来揭露一个严重妥协的锦平政府。

对于近平主席的拥护者来说，他缺乏连贯性并不重要，重要的是他们能够加入一个专注于一个人的事业。近平主席不是一个狂热分子。他的承诺既是自恋的，也是民族主义的。作为中国的新天子（天子），他与任何其他皇帝、国王、沙皇、元首或最高领袖都没有区别。他们都是一样的。

近平主席的劝诫是反对美国的霸权主义，他暗示美国打算让少数人对中国多数人实行暴政。狭隘地将美国描述为基督教将民族主义理想强加给世界其他地区，这让整个美国被刻板印象并描述为一种只能用武力对抗的文化。这也是美国福音派运动如此危险的众多原因之一。亚洲不同意这种世界观，而具有讽刺意味的是，特朗普是一个没有信仰的非信徒，已经被迫接受了它。近平主席，即使他想防止针对他认为的僵化的人性观点而采取的暴力行动，也并非没有道理，也无法阻止它。它会发生。

THE SUM OF ZERO - google translate

8

如果近平主席选择启动以武装力量为中心的战略，那么现在必须从他的傲慢的角度来考虑他对军队的影响。战争从来都不是谦卑地发起的。它没有认识到个人的重要性，低估了人的生命。它包含许多与群众运动的相似之处，因此也是一种强制工具。军队还为那些感到没有方向的人提供避难所。它还为雄心勃勃的人提供了机会。这是一种不容置疑的常规机制，因此为近平主席提供了许多巩固和维持控制权的选择。对于军队基层来说，他们捍卫中华人民共和国或专制总统并不重要。不愿让总司令不受制衡束缚的军事领导层将被取代。甚至被关进监狱。

人们不需要怀疑这种事件的可能性。威胁他会实施它。实施后，他将把中国变成一个军事独裁政权，而作为一个独裁者，他将保持对总统职位的控制，超出了他作为领导人的能力范围。这将在紧急情况的框架内完成。他将通过将军队释放到全球替罪羊身上来制造和制造紧急情况。毫无疑问，它将从小规模开始，但范围会扩大。历史上充斥着近期军事成功变成长期专制噩梦的例子。世界和平和中国繁荣将是受害者。一旦球开始滚动，无论多么无意，金平主席都无法阻止它。全世界都会联合起来反对他。他不是全知的，也不是全能的。他需要在冲动和好奇的自我放纵的框架内被考虑。共产党需要意识到，近平主席对中国和世界来说都是一个明显而现实的威胁。

为什么西方不表达持续的愤怒，并积极地将责任归咎于近平主席，这是一种懦弱的行为。他们是同谋，以至于他们允许贸易关系购买外交政策。近平主席是政治零和视角的产物，只要如此，美国就会继续处于风险之中。

美国已经被金钱在政治中的影响力所瘫痪，这些政治被标榜为国家服务。美国的代议制民主制度令人尴尬，但这并不意味着它会被一个叛徒、逃避征兵和被定罪的重罪犯的傀儡永久地蒙羞。另一方面，中国接受一位无法被罢免的领导人。他对他的国家所代表的威胁，远比目前由美国不完美的代议制民主选出的橙色小丑大得多。

正是近平主席对那些他觉得嘲笑的人的仇恨，他对中共自我实现的臃肿观念，才导致了他对美国政治的鄙视。他的蔑视为他提供了使用暴力的借口。近平主席将他的自恋转移到一种印象中，认为自己拥有只有他才能完成的使命——最危险的煽动者。把他塑造成一个荒谬的伪装者，一个玩弄儒家对领导的定义的人，这种定义是基于 尊重和信任的，假设一个明智的领导者会避免暴力，他们会谦虚并乐于接受他人的反馈，他们会努力寻求平衡，避免极端的自负。

恐惧滋生仇恨。想要滋生恐惧。当你意识到你非常想要的东西超出了你的掌握范围时，你的恐惧就会变成仇恨，而仇恨是所有情绪中最强大的，因为仇恨可以很容易地被骄傲合理化，而骄傲是所有罪恶中最致命的，因为它被用来合理化所有其他罪恶。

骄傲是对 自我的过度热爱。极端地说，这是对邻居的不尊重。骄傲包括夸大的自我重要性、过度关注自己以及不承认自己对上帝的依赖。谦卑带来智慧。骄傲带来了无知、贪婪、情欲、嫉妒和暴食。 骄傲总是预示着暴力和毁灭。过度自信和居高临下的傲慢以此为借口，为本来犯罪和不道德的行为辩护。这是每个民粹主义者的祸根。这些是金平主席和特朗普总统所表现出的品质，这些特质使他们特别不适合担任公职。

近平主席是关于恐惧和骄傲的教科书式案例。在他的内心深处，他觉得自己高人一等，当他意识到自己的目标处于危险之中时，他会让愤怒支配他的情绪，然后是报复和暴力的威胁。因为近平主席对自我的认知扭曲，他将对手重新定义为敌人，以证明他的骄傲是合理的。

他声称美国正在将他的对手作为武器的说法是无关紧要的。他必须提出极端的主张，以便创造一个可识别的目标，从中他可以灌输一种美国顽固腐败的信念。他煽动的仇恨对他来说不是可有可无的，但这也给金平主席带来了两难境地。特朗普可能具有侮辱性和不讨人喜欢的态度，但美国并非冷漠无情，尽管近平主席不断进行一连串的谩骂、谎言和侮辱，但这些霸凌策略虽然有时很有趣，但显得不成熟和绝望。

为了应对这种情况，美国需要做的就是继续表现出对中国苦难者的同情和支持。有市场价值的同理心活动，加上对持续进步的明确分析和建议，强调美国对中国文化体验的欣赏，将削弱近平的合法性。近平主席没有能力做同样的事情。否则，他将失去作为神圣的最高领袖的吸引力。差异将是明显的，而优势将归于特朗普。

关于如何削弱近平主席，需要设计一个有趣的推论来挑战他的支持者关注的单一问题——如何通过遵守近平主席定义的共产主义学说来确保获得机会。继续在男人身上播下怀疑的种子。这放松了国家主席近平对其支持者的控制，这需要通过表明西方高度重视中国公民，同时真正关心其国家主席的智慧的行动来补充。

特朗普需要将近平主席描述为一个令人讨厌的人物，对他来说，失败可以被视为战胜腐败的胜利和中国繁荣的胜利。将此与关注近平主席的外交纠葛以及他为普京和金正恩提供的支持联系起来。将近平主席的判断失误与他的公开声明联系起来，是削弱他攻击美国影响的必要条件。证明他们是心烦意乱的产物。这绝不能是对金平主席谎言的驳斥，因为他的谎言没有事实依据。相反，需要证明的是，这些声明旨在故意误导和制造恐惧和仇恨。表明近平主席的荒谬谩骂是缺乏纪律和尊重常识的严重误导的共产主义观点的产物。

近平主席是非理性的。他的不满缺乏事实依据，围绕着半真半假。他的抱怨很幼稚，以这种方式表明他迫切希望得到认可。具有讽刺意味的是，他对普京的赞美虽然令人震惊，但当人们考虑到他一定感到多么孤立时，这是可以理解的。他努力将自己政府的不足和失败转化为对外部影响的憎恨。近平主席对被美国孤立的领导人有一种天然的亲和力。毫无疑问，他也希望将这种孤立强加给美国的政治制度。

近平主席想象着对任何谴责他并让他相信自己的许多弱点的真理的强烈仇恨。习近平是一个极度缺乏安全感的人，正是他性格的这一方面导致他自我辩护。他是圣洁的，因为他需要如此。他嘲笑和伤害对手的愿望也是一种自我辩解的形式，他试图向他的追随者灌输这种态度。这种愤怒和仇恨只会在他内心滋生更多的蔑视，他用它来合理化对暴力的呼吁。从这个角度来看，金平主席很快就会失去对他所释放的情绪的控制。他将激发一种强烈的愿望，即拒绝外部对中国文化的影响。这种仇恨将滋生一种无耻，使那些受其困扰的人不受批评和争论的影响。

仇恨与嫉妒有着奇怪的联系。那些我们认为比我们更好的人比那些我们感到同情的人更容易被鄙视。近平总统觉得特朗普是他的下人，但知道特朗普觉得自己是老师。私下里，习嘲笑和惊叹这个男人的不成熟和无知。

长期以来，中国一直认为自己是最伟大的国家。这使中国在与其他国家进行比较时处于向内看的独特地位。这在中国造成了一种紧张关系，而美国特权的印象又加剧了这种紧张关系，而这种紧张关系更加矛盾，因为从某种意义上说，美国应该得到它的繁荣。

当美国人开始对美国梦失去信心时，他们也将开始将目光转向内部，试图将注意力集中在外部指责上。其他国家，尤其是中国，将被归咎于他们许多困难的根源。特朗普这个比喻的独特之处在于，他会把这与阴谋操纵人口的想法联系起来，作为旨在影响美国所享有的影响力的长期削弱的诡计。通过这种方式，他将进一步加剧这样一种观念，即美国的承诺和特权正在被一位纵容的中国总统从一个应得的工人阶级公民那里偷走。他的这个假设不会错。这是近平主席长期战略的一个公开和决定性因素——取代、主导和取代美国，成为这个工厂的杰出国家。

在近平主席身上，有一种对美国的崇敬。他在这里度过了一段时间，钦佩美国，在斥责美国犯下了最卑鄙的政治操纵形式时，他也在执行同样的事情。他声称他正在对抗政治，不是因为他认为我们的制度是腐败的，而是因为他试图挑衅。这具有将那些反对近平主席的人变成分身的效果。通过这种方式，整个政治外交被削弱和贬低，进一步证实了近平主席是国际对抗的危险推动者。

仇恨没有界限，会流向最有效的地方和反对派薄弱的地方。习近平制造的敌意为他的外交提供了动力，推动国家朝着他希望的遏制美国霸权的方向前进。这是一场危险的游戏，并且已经采取了低级侵略性的形式。不要怀疑，当暴力涉及到一个历史上感到委屈的中国时，暴力就会发生。最初的爆发点将发生在中国海，并最终导致对台湾的封锁。公海对抗是不可避免的，在某个时候，我们将看到首次在国际水域对美国海军中队使用低当量核武器。与中国的贸易将停止。地球将区域化，而太平洋上空的僵局将尘埃落定。战争不是靠战略取胜的。他们是通过消耗战赢得的。台湾将失去，但这将是近平主席结束的开始，因为他将面对一个与他作对的世界的生产力。唯一剩下的问题是，中国的过渡是会导致一个更加激进的好战政权，还是回归中国的协约国。

习近平的错误在于，国际社会的不妥协将严重损害中国。中国需要世界，世界也需要中国。如果中国在经济上受到伤害，它就有可能引起协调一致的公民不服从，并开始在全国范围内蔓延。这将预示着近平主席终结的开始。他的政权似乎无法妥协，并将消耗周围人的政治资本。如果内部冲突蔓延，他将以此为借口清洗他的队伍并投资于一个自动化监控社会。他将推动军国主义。事实上，他已经开始了这个过程，如上所述，这将使他能够在个人层面上平息异议。只要他能够实施这个控制计划，他就有足够的资金把中国变成一个奥威尔式的现实。不要怀疑，这将发生在一个已经完全缺乏隐私和个人选择的国家。对于近平主席来说，基于人工智能的自动化监控社会所提供的力量将是无法抗拒的。

近平主席的政权不仅想改变国家的方向，他们还想羞辱他们的对手。因此，他的复仇计划。他将从解除内部反对派的武装开始，更不用说像马云这样的创新者是这个国家的财富创造引擎。如果国家主席近平感到受阻，他将合法地想办法用武力来实施他的意志。为此，他将招募军队中柔韧的分子，如果他感到受到威胁，他会立即启动这些部队。对他来说，不容置疑的忠诚将变得比作为对原则的忠诚更重要。一旦这种专制制度在北京完全转移，其结果将是一个严厉惩罚和绝对臣服的社会。

近平主席是沙文主义的，这导致他变得残忍和没有同情心。他的不谦虚也滋生了一种自负和对他人的鄙视。这导致他居高临下和傲慢。因为近平主席认为自己是自我实现的，甚至是必要的，所以他认为自己没有责任。

他从对自己的行为的责任中解脱出来，就会变得冷酷无情，并赋予自己恐吓、撒谎、背叛甚至折磨的权力，而没有羞耻或自责。他的仇恨会自我强化。他已经无耻地歪曲了共产主义的治理理想。他贬低中国的异议，仿佛这是一种罪恶，以给人一种他是一位有能力的领导人的印象。他对堕落灵性的拟人化是他不断尝试将共产主义重新定义为个人使命的一个例子。

西蒙说，金平主席的竞选活动是政治性的。他的支持者被迫解释可能是真实的，但也可能是假的命令。近平主席利用这一点向他的追随者灌输默许，同时向他们灌输一种追随的观念。他通过要求不容置疑的忠诚来做到这一点，但他真正做的是要求别人模仿他的行为，以培养服从。这也使他的追随者免受外部影响。这在他们心中产生了一种虚假的自信，使他们坚定地支持他的事业。这种保证也在他们心中滋生了一种优越感，进而进一步激励他们效仿他们的领导者——一个让他们觉得自己有价值和目标的人。这就是习近平的基础如此坚韧的原因。

同质性孕育出统一性。千篇一律滋生了对外部影响的蔑视，因此构成了近平主席的基础如此凝聚力的另一个原因。这是一种与生俱来的反抗，进一步孤立了中国。习近平的信息是什么并不重要，重要的是他似乎以选民身份直接与他的支持者交谈。

让近平主席的角色变得可笑、令人尴尬和可悲，是让民众摆脱这种灌输所需要的。当对他的模仿不再为修正自我意识提供回报时，近平主席的支持者将再次产生一种他们被孤立、孤独和被遗忘的印象。这是他们最脆弱的时候，也最容易接受新事业的欢迎提案。

随着他们对这个人的奉献变得越来越优柔寡断，他的选民基础的凝聚力将变得脆弱，因此容易受到混淆、脱离、无序、分散和混淆近平主席信息的想法的影响。以男人本人的性格为中心的视觉效果。迷失方向的近平主席的信徒们将最容易接受那些将他们的注意力重新集中在一个新的、更有价值的任务上的信息。

近平主席的支持者故意不知情。他们不倾向于研究和确认他的性格和政策。事实上，这样做会浪费他们的时间。这样一来，整个中国在政治上都是不成熟的，极易受到自由职业者的影响。这在那些努力摆脱自我观念的人身上变得更加明显，在这种观念中，他们认为自己是应该受到谴责的个人失败。因为锦平的追随者故意好奇，而且缺乏获得信息资源的渠道，所以他们很容易被欺骗，这对总统来说既是强项也是弱项。这就是为什么习近平用重拳孤立中国。正是他对外部影响的不尊重和仇恨使他的国家与世界其他地区区分开来，这就是为什么美国必须努力产生对这个人的蔑视，而不是他的政策。

SMALL FRY - google translate
9

近平主席既不是一个伟大的沟通者，也不是一个三段论者。相反，他是一个扭曲的公关人员。因为他是一个宣传家，所以与其说他说服人，不如说把他的观点强加给人们。他们别无选择，只能"相信"。否则，他们将面临政府批准的监控所剥夺权利的脆弱性。这种奇特形式的确认偏见是金平主席用来操纵的，他的支持者想象阴谋集团正在努力压制它们，以便收编原本开明的观点。

国家主席近平正在引导他的信徒相信，暴力将是他恢复中国的必要步骤。合法化的恐怖就是从这种不宽容的蛹中产生的。不要怀疑，这将发生在一个仍然使用集中营镇压异见的国家。

近平主席的劝诱风格是强制性的，随着他的军队接近平等的拐点，我们会发现他的知识分子自负找到了越来越多的方法来忽视偏见并将动机合理化。总有一天，金平主席这个人、金平主席这个经理人，以及他作为共产主义伪装者的地位，会被一个自私自利的知识分子精英以反驳各方反对他的论点的名义合理化。走极端，它将被用来为这个人的行为开脱。毕竟，领导力和做出"艰难选择"的必要性何时会演变成犯罪。从道德角度来看，对于任何领导者来说，往往都会回归到可疑的倾向。当这些行为被孤立起来，在对与错的光明下看待时，这些行为就只是犯罪，往往被放大为反人类的罪行。这是任何专制政权所固有的巨大危险，一个不幸的特征，根植于被他之前的最高领导人合法化的金平主席政权中。

在中国，无知与智力并不矛盾，尽管坦率地说，这是许多有成就的知识分子经常遇到的情况，这可能是骄傲的合理化力量的结果。对于许多中国人来说，这将是源于自私、嫉妒和贪婪的简单愚昧行为，被合理化为知识分子忠诚的功德榜样。

近平主席预示着利用权力来维持总统任期。这个国家迅速崛起的激进分子也接受了这种军事化的马克思主义的思想。需要根据每个人的能力和每个人的枪支来清除国际政治中所谓的腐烂，首先是驱逐那些毒害了曾经在 **Sino Manifest Destiny** 授权下组织的中国东方伟大霸权的文化神圣性的人。

近平主席认为，阻止中国屈服与将自己提升为中国共产主义事业无懈可击的冠军密不可分。这样，西方将金平描绘成一个大骗子，将人们束缚和蒙蔽在他的意志中，这一点至关重要。使用法西斯主义的描述是不恰当的，必须谨慎使用，但必须这样做。国家主席近平可能会因使用图像而受损，这些图像会让中国人对他的意图感到恐惧。在一个被压抑的共产主义中国，内战总是指日可待。

近平主席的信息令人发指，其根源在于他在农村的成长经历。然而，由于中国对特权进行了分层，这已经面临风险，现在人们认为这种特权正受到国内移民稀释影响的日益威胁。正是这种感知到的优势丧失，促使国家主席近平收紧了控制。党派关系的另一面是特权。在中国，特权也经常是种族主义的。近平主席认识到了这一点，但将其转变为根除维吾尔人、哈萨克族和吉尔吉斯族以及宗教少数群体成员的文化认同的借口——其根源在于压制自由理念，以支持同质化和不宽容的民族主义中共经验。

民粹主义者的性格是什么？他们好斗、本能、有动力、有目的、对自己的直觉有把握，但他们也是放荡的、挥霍的、不道德的、可耻的、无耻的和挥霍的。这是否描述了金平主席？

每个时代都包含自己独特的法西斯主义味道。自封的皇帝、党主席和终身主席都围绕着一个绝对无误的领导人的理念，在这一点上，锦平主席也不例外。这种类型的自恋者之所以受欢迎，并不是因为相信他们代表了最好的公民身份，而是源于对政治和政府现状的深深不满。没有这种挫败感，这种类型的领导者只不过是一个不谦虚的活动家和吹牛者。

英帝国主义的耻辱和鸦片战争为中国社会的分裂奠定了基础，并为军事化的日本法西斯侵略中国开辟了道路。然后，蒋介石必然花费中国的政治凝聚力来对抗侵略者，这使得中国无法抵抗毛的政治感染。

这种对内的关注分散了中国对紧迫社会问题的注意力，并将资源重新分配给基于非理性的共产主义原则的无可归属的利益，就像苏联的情况一样，这最终集中在内部警务和军事能力投资上，以抵御想象中的外国威胁。在向中央集权经济的最初过渡期间，中国没有获得任何好处，这场嘲讽变成了难以想象的规模的悲剧，也为创作了对共产主义的漫画模仿——近平主席——提供了基础。从这个角度来说，他就是中共政治经历的偶然。要把他赶下台，就需要重新把注意力放在中国民众的需求和优先事项上，首先要强调繁荣和自决的原则。

近平主席不是一个拥有无与伦比的智慧的人。他是一个生活在个人崇拜外表后面的人，他能够以惊人的无视礼仪戒律的方式将仇恨合法化。也许有人认为他对人性有精打细算的洞察力，但这种给他贴上政治专家标签的倾向，对于一个洞察力如此有限的人来说，这种赞誉实在是太慷慨了。难以言喻的宏伟与不敬的自信相结合，是近平主席用来用坚定的目标取代其支持者中存在的卑鄙卑鄙的东西。他正乘着一股民族主义自豪感的浪潮，他将自己独特的性格缺陷附加到这股浪潮上。他是一个当下的人，很快就会发现那些取笑他的人的奉承中蕴含着现成的傲慢。直到他们发现他们可以摆脱对他影响力的不满。

近平主席的政策尚未演变成一种公开的法西斯主义形式，但他正在不可阻挡地朝着这个方向前进。当他采用他的政权特有的新标志时，他将表明他已经到来。到那时，他将把自己变成共产主义经验的英雄嘲讽者，这将表明他打算以加强人民共和国的名义颠覆马克思主义原则并实施少数人的暴政。

他的副手们的耻辱在于，他们让自己被一个伟大领袖的形象所迷惑，而这位领袖最终会摧毁他们所有人。必须尝试将他们的懦弱转化为恐惧，担心他们最终会在金平主席的忠诚祭坛上被牺牲。他们内心对这个男人有一种愤怒的怨恨，可以用来散播对习近平人品的怀疑。

近平主席似乎确实有能力以平淡无视惯例的方式粉饰无耻的指示。虽然之前的 **20** 世纪民粹主义者表现出狂热，但近平主席的这一特征似乎是对狭隘无知和他自己膨胀的自我价值感的奴隶式承诺。这个男人的包装是如此令人反感，以至于他必须在他的追随者眼中显得荒谬。他是一个品牌，也是一个傲慢的例子，如果它符合他的目的，他就会诉诸暴力。

金平主席的领导风格更令人惊讶的表现之一是他性格的坚忍不拔，以及他言论的乏味内容。由于他的想法荒谬不合逻辑，他必须绝对肯定地宣布它们。他必须以无拘无束的自信来传达自己的想法，因为对他的支持者来说，重要的是大头大姿态，他对他人意见的蔑视，以及他对相反证据的蔑视。他们利用这一点来摆脱他们自己缺乏原创思维的想法。

近平主席知道自己是个骗子。所有共产党员都是，但在某些方面，这是品牌营销的核心。他的支持者要求他有条不紊地歪曲事实。这也是为什么金平主席如此公然地指责他的反对者犯下了他所犯的同样的事情。他称美国政府是一种耻辱，有时确实如此，因为他经常被公开指责。在某种程度上，甚至对他自己来说，他也是没有定义的。他是一个空壳，里面装满了对现实的反应性歪曲，这样他就可以保护自己免受无关紧要的影响。

他的谩骂毫无意义，而且因为它们没有事实依据，所以不能用事实来攻击它们。唯一可以用来反驳他经常荒谬的评论的回应是，它们是不真实的，它们是谎言，而且没有证据表明这些指控在现实中存在。在这一点上，争论只是变成了怀疑，而近平主席的大部分声明则完好无损。这就是为什么必须攻击这个人本人，而不是他的论点。如果他的形象被削弱，他的虚假陈述就会开始动摇。近平主席是另一种事实的不协调。这些矛盾注入了他的个性，因此使他特别容易受到人物解构的影响。将他的个性推销为对这个人本人空虚本性的难以置信的揭露。他与他的政策的联系将立即开始瓦解。

近平主席的追随者们在轻松放弃独立思考中找到了解脱。他们没有安全感，因此有一种天生的追随倾向。对于金平主席的崇拜者来说，自由和自由是在他们作为他的追随者之一的地位平等中实现的。他们对集体企业的承担感到满足。这就是为什么如果近平主席失败了，他的追随者会茫然地回头看着任何关于他们也是罪魁祸首的指责，因为在他们看来，这是一项政治化的努力，他们没有承担任何个人责任。因此，他们将渴望追随下一个原因，对前一个原因毫无羞耻感。指责近平的支持者会适得其反，毫无意义。他们把责任归咎于近平主席本人。对他们来说，他做什么并不重要，重要的是他们被他引导。他们无偿的牺牲将是习近平的回报。

作为领导人，邓小平和近平主席之间的主要区别是什么？邓小平认为，他有责任释放中国政治集体的创新精神和智慧，以支持支持国家追求繁荣和幸福的任务。另一方面，近平主席认为，有些人必须为支持党政策的人受苦。他相信，所有的人最终都会追求对他们最好的东西，而忽略了大多数人的需求。他的愿景要求将奖励按比例分配给最值得的人，而这取决于对他的事业的服从。这个概念认为，所有男人在任其设计时，最终都会追求对他们最好的东西，而不管它对他人的影响如何。毫无疑问，近平主席已经采用了这种人性观点。他是一个反常的自恋者，因此觉得自己是最值得的。他将贪婪地追求荣誉、权力和建立一个王朝，这个王朝的任务是仅凭他的意志力量来维持他心目中注定的事件。

天安门大屠杀不是随机事件。虽然近平主席不打算重演这一悲剧，但他正在努力通过在社区层面对民众进行有针对性的控制和监视来防止这种必要性。这是他需要保持对自己作为傀儡和领导者的关注的必然结果。这是因为他对顺从的呼吁是为了巩固和再次确认他对民粹主义者的承诺。如果近平主席没有发起这一坚持党的政策的呼吁，他的选民基础就会瓦解，他就不会成为今天这个毫无反对派的利安德。这就是为什么他不可避免地会诉诸暴力作为共和国之外的行动。这是任何民粹主义者保持承诺所需的必要部分。对于金平主席的信徒来说，这一行动呼吁在他们心中创造了一种舒适的同志情谊，这种情谊使他们能够在他们认为比自己更伟大的事业中迷失自我。

必须记住，中国政治棘手的困境是公民的冷漠，这种冷漠在无奈中显露出来，即国家将他们从选择的负担中解放出来，但也将他们从个人责任中解放出来。目前的结果是，他们对党员特权的热情超过了对自决所带来的承诺的热情。西方需要通过煽动对近平主席的厌恶来让他们摆脱冷漠。将中国最糟糕的一面与近平主席的政权联系起来。提供社会不公正、党派腐败和不平等医疗保健的无数例子，其中中国的肥胖已经消耗了医疗保健预算的1/5。以及由党的政策导致的破产，工人在不可预测的市场中失去了一切。

证明这一切都是在允许富人无尽机会逃避他们对国家的义务的框架内完成的。

将这一点与共产主义政策联系起来是很容易的。**Hammer** 指出，共产党利用其办公室来充实自己。积极地将他们与他们出售给他人的人情联系起来。做更多的事情，而不仅仅是提供虐待的数字说明。将视觉效果附加到他们的财富积累示例，例如房屋、船只、飞机等。将滥用中国财政制度与操纵外国投资、政府资助的产业和基础设施投资联系起来。近平主席的支持者对此知之甚少，会感到受到虐待。证明他远非希望让系统变得更好，而是维护权力并系统性地滥用系统以谋取私利。

美国必须把近平主席塑造成一个被忽视的腐败的有害瘴气。证明共产党的关注点不是人，而是维护特权。以腐败的政治局为例，说明滥用权力一直到最高层。表明是时候为总统和最高领导人推出任期限制提案了。提出弹劾机制，将腐败的中国领导人赶下台。近平主席是一个不受约束的独裁者。除非这种情况发生改变，否则整个中国，乃至全世界，都将处于危险之中。

近平主席的支持者有时看起来顽固无遗、刀枪不入，但实际上，只要他们认为自己是成功的变革推动者，他们就背负着给近平主席及其政权带来毁灭的种子。批评者说习近平、共产党和他收编的政治局腐败是不够的。他们贪污的视觉例子必须附在他们身上，即使他们试图将自己描绘成以服务国家的名义做出牺牲。这里的目标是空洞的普通中国公民，他们仍然可以被证明他们实际上被解雇和辱骂。证明对权力的限制和外交政策的开放性是为他们提供唯一真正救赎的机会。

近平主席的受益者被恐惧所淹没。他们的自我贬低表现在他们对党外其他人的担忧上。习近平利用这一点让他的支持者和追随者对他们在他的等级制度中的地位处于持续的焦虑状态。他对党内批评者的诋毁造成了恐惧，并孤立了对政策的批判性评价。其目的是将他们作为对这项事业的牺牲，以保持忧虑处于狂热的程度。目标是保持对近平主席理念的无可置疑的忠诚。

放弃原则带来的分裂进一步孤立了近平爱好者。这是危险的，因为它为仇恨的加速提供了基础，而通过这种方式，近平主席的受益者在他们的承诺上变得更加极端。随着他们承诺的强度增加，他们对西方民主国家，特别是美国的厌恶将会增加，以至于他们对替代治理体系的接受变得不可持续——这是暴力的前奏。

当这种情况发生时，普通中国公民将完全放弃他们选择的权力或任何不同意这个人本人的倾向，即使是私下里。他们会觉得自己仿佛已经从变幻莫测的政治制度中解脱出来。然后，他们将抓住国家主席近平的种族优越计划，努力压制异议。当这种情况发生时，它们将被用来将国家转变为中国帝国专制政权的军国主义冠军。

浪费一个开明的知识分子中国词典，才是金平主席的真正悲剧。他歪曲了原则。但是，如果说中共的实验被污染了，那是因为金钱在共产主义中的腐败影响。近平主席就是由此产生的毒瘤。如果不是他，那肯定是别人。

近平主席的残忍是一种经批准的胁迫形式，他理所当然地必须诋毁美国的法学体系，以切断中国与美国的联系，这是一个理想的选择。只要他能够保持对中国制度的信心，并将变革重新定义为现代化，公众就不会接受对国家主席近平政策的激进拒绝。西方必须将锦屏描述为口是心非、危险甚至妄想。这里的危险在于，这会诱使他做出暴力反应，但如果这种情况能够得到控制，就会削弱他的政府。它甚至可能是可取的，因为它会引发如此严重的离经叛道的反应，以至于他可能看起来对中国民族主义理想不忠。

对西方民主国家来说，一个相关的危险是，近平有效地利用了妥协的行动者来为他的政策提供动力。将这个人与这些去合法化者联系起来，并证明他们自己也被妥协了。他们是男人和女人，将自己与共产主义的模仿联系起来，试图获得权力和积累财富。向中国公众表明，他们作为党内享有特权和腐败的元素存在于中国之外。一个将自己的道德卖给一个没有正直、良知或道德的人的政党。

此外，美国必须努力将一个富有表现力的近平支持者子群体与整体区分开来。这部分共产党需要一个借口来转移支持。通过不适当的政策的具体例子来诱导这一点，然后承认这些政策是不可持续的。一个很好的例子是，一个完全、而不是部分和公平地资助的教育和医疗保健系统。对服务的访问不受限制。这需要被描绘成党的一个有目的的视角。对普通中国公民的故意抛弃。

美国甚至可以承认，近平主席说关税对两国都有伤害是正确的。关税是半场网球。特朗普没有考虑到的是，球场上有两支球队和另一名球员。（历史学家莎拉·潘恩（Sarah Paine）使用的比喻）例如，1930 年，美国通过了 Smoot-Hawley 法案，以保护美国的就业和制造业。没有预料到的是这对日本的影响，日本随后被限制与美国进行贸易。日本随后将帝国主义视为替代方案。1 年后，日本将进攻满洲，剩下的就是历史了。生活（和国际贸易）是一种互动。特朗普的和解姿态没有提到习，而是考虑到关税对美国和中国人口的影响，这可能会赢得许多人的支持，并重要的是削弱习。我们需要记住，中国渴望得到认可和尊重。承认中国的担忧，同时拒绝将近平主席视为一个可悲且不值得模仿的人。在情感上，将近平担任总统与当他将支持转向普京、金正恩和伊朗时中国将遭受损失的确定性联系起来。将乌克兰的斗争描绘成与台湾争取自决的斗争有相似之处的斗争。利用这一点来证明近平主席是一个政治者，需要阻止他使中国远离与美国和世界的富有成效的关系。

习近平渴望威望和崇拜。他的虚荣心驱使他渴望不断地重新确认这一地位，这就是最初驱使他从政的原因。我们需要记住的是，他对待批评是个人的。如果他感到不被尊重，这会刺激他更卑鄙的情绪。

近平主席所赢得的宽容远远超出了他作为政治家的能力范围。看到一些知识分子对一个如此洞察力有限的人赞不绝口，真是令人痛心。他们向他投掷赞美，希望他能赐予他们豁免。相反，他们会发现他们的忠诚会被揭示为迂腐和不被欣赏。

习近平扭曲了中国神话。美国需要在西方对中国伟大的视角中创造一种恢复的信仰和钦佩。至少，它会让近平主席的支持者感到困惑，他们自然而然地被这些想法所吸引。在最好的情况下，它将揭示总统是一个对误导比领导更感兴趣的宣传者。无知永远不能被诋毁，只会变得可笑和值得嘲笑。

西方需要记住，加在中国身上的羞辱是真实的，需要通过具体的外交和解来解决。被独裁者所吸引的民众的担忧是真实的担忧，在媒体影响者的推动和拉扯中，这些担忧是不能忽视的，他们赞成优先考虑总统的担忧，而不是中国国内和国际政策造成的不平衡。

近平主席正在做的，就是为一个明显不那么宽容的中国奠定基础。他首先诋毁了他所说的反华族裔。他通过制造怀疑使中国漂泊不定，然后将自己作为幻灭者的救生筏。他用歪曲共产主义理想的口号和信仰准则来支持自己的承诺

他的反对派已经失去了抵抗他的意愿。西方民主国家希望中国出口驱动型经济的优先事项能够控制近平，但会发现他已经将这一当务之急纳入了总统职位。中国与世界的关系已经被强加了一个新的秩序。习近平将要做的是放开一个在国际关系中强加不妥协和对抗制度的进程。金平不会

在乎。到那时，他对中国主导的太平洋地区的愿景将接替他。

需要记住的是，习近平的选民希望废除他们的权威，转而采用一人结构领导的一党制解决方案。他们不渴望个人自由，而是希望将自己与目标的同质性保持一致，这将对抗他们认为的碎片化政府体系中的弱点。美国必须用权威声明来反击这一点，表明美国可以在适当和需要的时候行使经济和道德权威。这样做的前提是认识到，必须通过修改共产主义正统观念所定义的限制来尊重中国的经验。

THE SNAKE HAS LEGS - google translate

10

让我们称它们为它们。难以理解的白痴，他们中的很多人，从政治局里许多愚蠢的共产党代表开始。他们接受了一个国家主席的纲领，这个纲领利用非理性来暗示他有明确的目标。近平主席在原本值得称赞的共产主义共同体原则中加入了资本主义的附属品，他用这些附属品来强化这样一种观念，即他是一位在适当的时候被适当定位的领导人，可以为国家带来秩序。他所做的只是用罪孽来覆盖平等。

习近平似乎是一个在好奇心方面存在独特缺陷的人。当你把这一点与他奇怪的无法体验到同理心结合起来时，你会发现习近平是一个特别没有好奇心的人。再加上极度的自恋，他特别不适合领导中华民族。他的自恋确实为他提供了一种特殊的指责和谴责能力，这两种品质在沉思思想领域不需要太多。一个有趣的推论是，他的支持者也希望得到同样的愿望——一个不需要太多自我反省的异议计划。这是他们避免确认他们值得被定罪的一种方式。

习近平对党的迅速控制的另一个有趣方面是，他的极端已经开始在党的框架中制造裂缝。异议已经开始感染队伍。他的支持者彼此为敌，这促使他们在试图与总统保持一致时走向极端。这只会进一步破坏近平主席为了维持其职位而需要传达的信息和目标的稳定性。虽然他的支持不太可能有意义地流失，但他希望保持对自己地位的控制会减弱。他越是试图控制自己的信息，信息就会变得越不合理，而这正是放松他对权力的控制所需要强调的。

近平主席最大的弱点是近平主席本人。他不可避免地会妨碍他自己的方式。他的声明试图实用，但实际上是不合逻辑和极端的。不过，他的观察的直接性有时可能出奇地具有先见之明。美国确实需要承认，中国的政治经验是合理的，即使它不利于民主多元。

但这并不意味着习近平的大部分政策都是适当的。如果普京攻击乌克兰是不行的。驱逐不受欢迎的种族是不道德的。否认西藏自治是一种荒谬。拒绝台湾的自决权就是帝国主义。他的言论给人一种既冲动又非理性的无纪律的头脑，这预示着他的政策将变得越来越不稳定。用它来对付他。不幸的是，他不妥协的管理风格也使他的不可预测性变得危险。他缺乏重新评估和妥协的能力，如果他继续执政，他的行动几乎肯定会开始瓦解中国与世界互补的一体化。

近平主席的首要任务不是合作重塑中国与世界的关系，而是获得这种关系。他的目标将转向延长和巩固他对权力的控制。起初，为了转移削弱他地位的企图，结果将是使他的罢免变得更加困难的规则。通过这种方式，他将创造一个事实上的中国王权。毛的终身任期已经在重演，中国文化体验的活力将被阉割。不要怀疑近平主席会尝试这样做，他已经开始了选举权。

中国宪法宣誓于 2016 年 1 月 1 日实施。如果近平主席试图将自己插入誓言中以明确忠诚，我们将知道他打算用新的近平主席个人崇拜来取代共产主义机构。如果他用个人象征来补充这一点，我们可以确信他正在试图复制国家社会主义的过度行为。最后，如果这是通过人工智能管理的整合和破坏国家传统行政结构来实现的，中国将变成一个寡头盗贼统治。

我们将看到贪婪和野心围绕这位总统具体化，从他的个人和家庭财富开始。温顺的人将被剥夺继承权，在新的中国政治框架中变得无关紧要。

令人感兴趣的是，近平主席是否发现他需要求助于军队来维持社会控制。如果异议失控，他将制造或升级地方危机，以此将注意力从他办公室的失败上转移开。当他这样做时，他将援引一种国家当务之急，将共产主义注入一种恢复秩序的半宗教义务中。他会编造一个借口，要求他施加紧急权力来动员军队。有趣的是，医疗大流行将令人钦佩地达到这一目的。在国际上，扩大的空军和海军，辅以海外港口和空军基地，然后用于覆盖主要贸易路线，也可以实现将中国的不满情绪从内部挑战中转移出来的目标。

近平主席的政府注定会令人不快和士气低落。他会冷酷无情，自鸣得意。如有必要，他将准备牺牲他的同志来维持他对权力的控制，并在此过程中牺牲中国的机构来巩固控制。事实上，他已经与中国学术界合作了。

近平主席留下的遗产将是一段停滞和物价上涨的时期，因为他浪费了中国在技术和劳动力方面的比较优势。他将把 IT 时代的杠杆变成监控机制，并以安全和遵守法治的名义实施控制。对基础设施的投资将转变为军事化的虚荣项目。像这样的共产党安全网将被漏洞所覆盖，这些漏洞有利于精英，同时放弃其余精英。

我们可以想象，广阔的军事项目将捕捉到他自恋的想象力，作为他自己膨胀的自我价值感的表达。中国的贫困地区将被转变为隔离的排斥区和政府控制区。监狱系统将扩大并变异成古拉格。就像他之前的斯大林和希特勒一样，转型后的惯犯官僚机构将成为他更顽固的反对者的便利垃圾场。

近平主席并不是一个异类。他是被帝国主义和战争破坏的中国政治经验的产物，现在被金钱的腐败影响所支配。如果不加以控制，他将成为第一个中国法西斯主义者和这个星球上的第一个 AI 独裁者。

在他自己看来，金平主席认为自己就是答案。具有讽刺意味的是，他将扼杀创造力，并将中国的精力投入到经济帝国主义、殖民化和战争中。社交媒体将变成国际战争的工具。窃取的技术将被武器化，共产主义将被转化为祥神。

他将努力取代美元成为主要商业货币，并利用在岸生产能力方面的优势来操纵外交政策。当时机成熟时，他将考虑用他持有的 7500 亿美元国债操纵美国债券市场，以破坏美国货币和经济的稳定。

他将创造一种新的中国数字货币。一个具有隐含监视能力的。经济将下放，需要在国家层面进行进一步的监督和控制，这一发展可能会演变为对更多控制的呼吁，并最终将整个中国经济军事化。如果经济步履蹒跚，战争将被用来重振国家。转变为寡头垄断的企业集团将成为政府的重点。世界将重新战壕，以应对习近平主席任期的这种孤立表现。此后不久，将开始对世界剩余经济体及其相关资源的控制和联邦化的争夺。太空与被军事化。局部低等级冲突将很快接踵而至。

然后，国家主席近平将转向诋毁犹太教-基督教。他将用发动战争的能力淹没非洲，这将激发进一步的努力来影响资源垄断。欠中国的债务将被用来操纵外交政策。这将在这些地区爆发军事冲突的那一天启动。金平主席是世界末日的预兆吗？这并不是不可能的。近平主席的总统任期即将在全世界的转折点上发展。他的印记将印在随后的一切上，一种对人类未来的近平主席大锤效应，有可能带来悲剧。

不祥的暗示是，一个军事化的中国将变成一个巨大的武器车间——一个专制的军火库。共产主义和军事化的民族主义将公然融合，并采取不可抗拒的行动紧迫性，这将威胁到文明，并诱使中国将修改后的中国共产主义昭示命运概念强加给世界。

如果有机会产生希望，它可能取决于世界激发中国的兴趣，即向欢迎融入国际社会所提供的巨大可能性开放。普通中国公民不再习惯于严重的困难。**Sacrifice for Party** 现在只不过是陈词滥调。中国人民已经准备好在国际上表达自己，如果有机会，他们将以开放的心态去表达自己。世界上伟大的经济民主国家可以为他们提供道路。

反对国家主席近平，这与令人信服的目标确定性和承诺的力量有关，将赢得胜利。这可以解释为文化停滞不前的中国社会对极右翼伪共产党的诅咒的重新觉醒。康复、改革和恢复。这些想法只需要容纳和认识到中国文化体验是多元的、强大的，并通过承认其内在的多元性而得到加强。

美国已经并将继续受益于移民的恢复性好处。它在经济、文化和现在的技术上革新了这个国家。移民在许多方面防止了美国停滞不前。多样性是它的巨大优势。这就是为什么美国更希望欢迎中国移民的原因。将中国人对 **Zouxiam**

的描述改为移民到美国所需的道路，以迎接机会。承认 1882 年《排华法案》的错误，并通过 2025 年《华人包容法案》。 <u>人才流失中国</u>。仅此一项就可以减少战争的可能性，并将焦点放在近平主席身上，认为这是共产党国内政策的一个错误。这些侨民将激励美国并激励国际社会热情地接受中国全球公民带来的好处。它还将有效制衡中国向同质化迈进的步伐。

可以理解的是，随着中国的现代化，它经历了城市与农村、工人阶级与上层阶级之间的分歧。相反，美国能做的是利用这种差距，欢迎活力和可能性的创造性爆炸，这改变了作为一个不受束缚的中国公民在世界上表达自己的意义。这将稳定中国文化体验这一现象，它将刷新作为中国人的意义。西方民主国家现在可以从现在开始，认识到中国的孤立和对表达的渴望，以此作为对不被欣赏的中国公民的救赎之路。

针对国家主席习近平的案件必须被积极起诉。他是一个不断发展的法西斯主义者和一个有抱负的帝国主义者。他的目标是历史报复，至少他必须在国际上陷入僵局。让共产党摆脱自满。中国仍然可以成为未来的财富创造引擎。另一种选择是华人血统回到教条主义的黑暗中。世界将热情欢迎、吸收和采用中国文化体验的盛开。辛勤工作的男男女女是中国经济奇迹的中坚力量，他们的创造性活力曾经是邓小平发起的"北京之春"的重要组成部分。他们可以再次这样做，以造福全人类。

中国 – 仰望孩子的纯真和巨大潜力，然后原谅并与世界和平相处。

www.ingramcontent.com/pod-product-compliance
Lightning Source LLC
Chambersburg PA
CBHW051550250726

48653CB00004BA/1078